TEACHER'S PET PUBLICATIONS

PUZZLE PACK
for
The Pigman

based on the book by
Paul Zindel

Written by
William T. Collins

© 2005 Teacher's Pet Publications
All Rights Reserved

The materials in this packet are copyrighted
by Teacher's Pet Publications, Inc.

These pages may be duplicated by the purchaser
for use in the purchaser's own classroom.

Copying any of these materials and distributing them
for any other purpose is a violation of the copyright laws.

© 2005 Teacher's Pet Publications, Inc.
www.tpet.com

INTRODUCTION
If you already own the LitPlan for this title, this Puzzle Pack will refresh your Unit Resource Materials and Vocabulary Resource Materials sections plus give you additional materials you can substitute into the tests. If you do not already have a complete LitPlan, these pages will give you some supplemental materials to use with your own plan. There are two main groups of materials: one set for unit words (such as characters' names, symbols, places, etc.) and one set for vocabulary words associated with the book.

WORD LIST
There is a word list for both the unit words and the vocabulary words. These lists show you which words are being used in the materials and the clues or definitions being used for those words. You may want to give students a word list with clues/definitions to help them, or you may want students to only have a word list (without clues/definitions) if you want them to work a little harder. Both are available for duplication. The word lists can also be your "calling key" for the bingo games.

FILL IN THE BLANK AND MATCHING
There are 4 each of the fill in the blank and matching worksheets for both the unit and vocabulary words. These pages can be used either as extra worksheets for students or as objective parts of a unit test. They can be done individually if students need extra help or as a whole class activity to review the material covered.

MAGIC SQUARES
The magic squares not only reinforce the material covered but also work on reasoning and math skills. Many teachers have told us that their students really enjoy doing these!

WORD SEARCH PUZZLES
The word search words go in all directions, as indicated on your answer keys. Two of the word search puzzles have the clues listed rather than the words. This makes the puzzle a little more difficult, but it reinforces the material better. Two word search puzzles have words only for students who find the clue puzzles too difficult.

CROSSWORD PUZZLES
Both unit and vocabulary word sections have 4 crossword puzzles.

BINGO CARDS
There are 32 individual bingo cards for the unit words and 32 individual bingo cards for the vocabulary words. You can use your word list as a "call list," calling the words at random and marking them off of your list as you go, or you could use the flash cards by cutting them apart and drawing the words at random from a hat (or box or whatever). To make a better review, you might ask for the definition and spelling of each word as you call it out–or you could call out the definitions and have students tell you the words they need to look for on the puzzle.

JUGGLE LETTERS
The vocabulary juggle letter game is intended to help students learn the spellings of the words. One sheet has the definitions listed on it as an extra help for students who need it or to reinforce the definitions if you choose to do so.

FLASH CARDS
We've included a set of vocabulary flash cards you can duplicate, cut, and fold for your students. Some teachers make a few sets for general use by the class; others make a set for each student. Some teachers duplicate them for each student and have the students cut & fold their own. You can cut out just the words and put them in a hat, have each student pick out one word and write the definition and a sentence for that word. Students then swap words and papers, with the next student adding a sentence of his own under the last one. You can have students swap as many times as you like. Each time the student will read the sentences written prior to his own and then add a sentence. You can cut out the words and definitions separately and play "I Have; Who Has?" Each student in the room draws a word and definition. The first student says, "I have (the name of the word). Who has the definition?" The student with the definition reads it then says, "I have (the name of the vocabulary word she has). Who has the definition?" The round continues until all words and definitions have been given.

The Pigman Word List

No.	Word	Clue/Definition
1.	AHRA	Aunt whose ghost gets blamed
2.	ALBERT	The prince in a can
3.	ALICE	Dear ___
4.	ANGELO	Mr. Pignati's first name
5.	ASSASSIN	Money
6.	ATTACK	Mr. Pignati had a heart ___
7.	BARON	___ Park Zoo
8.	BOATMAN	Magic
9.	BOBO	A baboon
10.	BOMBER	Bathroom ___
11.	BORE	The ___; John's father
12.	CHECK	Mr. Pignati gave the L&J fund one for $10
13.	CONCHETTA	Mrs. Pignati. She's not in California.
14.	CRICKET	The librarian
15.	DEANNA	She fixed the attendance cards for L & J
16.	DELICACIES	What Mr. Pignati buys J & L to eat
17.	DENNIS	School friend of John & Lorraine
18.	ELECTRICIAN	Mr. Pignati's former occupation
19.	FUND	The L & J ___
20.	HOWARD	Avenue; Mr. Pignati's street
21.	HUSBAND	Love
22.	KENNETH	John's older brother
23.	KING	'Old maid' English teacher
24.	KOBIN	Dennis's last name
25.	LATIN	Club Lorraine used as an excuse for not being home
26.	LONELY	These people need visitors
27.	LOVER	Sex
28.	MARSHMALLOW	___ Kid; Norton
29.	NORTON	Has a habit of shoplifting
30.	ODDBALL	... get your hair cut. You look like an ___.
31.	OLD	John's mother: ___ Lady
32.	OMENS	Peanut lady, peacock, & nocturnal room were ___ of a bad day
33.	PEACOCK	Lorraine was attacked by a low IQ ___
34.	PEANUTS	Food for Bobo
35.	PIGMAN	Mr. Pignati
36.	PIGS	What Mr. Pignati collects
37.	ROLL	Supercolossal fruit ___
38.	SKATING	Roller rink activity at Mr Pignati's house
39.	TELEPHONE	___ marathon
40.	TOMB	Masterson's ___
41.	TONY	___'s market; sells beer to anyone
42.	WALL	Street where Kenneth works
43.	WIFE	Fun
44.	ZOO	Bobo's home

The Pigman Fill In The Blanks 1

_____

1. Dennis's last name
2. _____ marathon
3. Money
4. Peanut lady, peacock, & nocturnal room were ___ of a bad day
5. Mr. Pignati gave the L&J fund one for $10
6. Club Lorraine used as an excuse for not being home
7. The prince in a can
8. The L & J ___
9. John's older brother
10. Mr. Pignati's former occupation
11. John's mother: ___ Lady
12. Aunt whose ghost gets blamed
13. Has a habit of shoplifting
14. These people need visitors
15. ____ Kid; Norton
16. Sex
17. School friend of John & Lorraine
18. Mrs. Pignati. She's not in California.
19. Fun
20. Street where Kenneth works

The Pigman Fill In The Blanks 1 Answer Key

KOBIN	1. Dennis's last name
TELEPHONE	2. _____ marathon
ASSASSIN	3. Money
OMENS	4. Peanut lady, peacock, & nocturnal room were ___ of a bad day
CHECK	5. Mr. Pignati gave the L&J fund one for $10
LATIN	6. Club Lorraine used as an excuse for not being home
ALBERT	7. The prince in a can
FUND	8. The L & J ___
KENNETH	9. John's older brother
ELECTRICIAN	10. Mr. Pignati's former occupation
OLD	11. John's mother: ___ Lady
AHRA	12. Aunt whose ghost gets blamed
NORTON	13. Has a habit of shoplifting
LONELY	14. These people need visitors
MARSHMALLOW	15. ____ Kid; Norton
LOVER	16. Sex
DENNIS	17. School friend of John & Lorraine
CONCHETTA	18. Mrs. Pignati. She's not in California.
WIFE	19. Fun
WALL	20. Street where Kenneth works

The Pigman Fill In The Blanks 2

_____
_____
_____
_____
_____
_____
_____
_____
_____
_____
_____
_____
_____
_____
_____
_____
_____
_____
_____
_____

1. Fun
2. ... get your hair cut. You look like an ___.
3. Avenue; Mr. Pignati's street
4. Peanut lady, peacock, & nocturnal room were ___ of a bad day
5. A baboon
6. These people need visitors
7. Mr. Pignati had a heart ___
8. Food for Bobo
9. The prince in a can
10. Street where Kenneth works
11. ___'s market; sells beer to anyone
12. Club Lorraine used as an excuse for not being home
13. Mrs. Pignati. She's not in California.
14. Mr. Pignati gave the L&J fund one for $10
15. Sex
16. The L & J ___
17. Mr. Pignati's former occupation
18. Love
19. Lorraine was attacked by a low IQ ___
20. Mr. Pignati

The Pigman Fill In The Blanks 2 Answer Key

WIFE	1. Fun
ODDBALL	2. ... get your hair cut. You look like an ___.
HOWARD	3. Avenue; Mr. Pignati's street
OMENS	4. Peanut lady, peacock, & nocturnal room were ___ of a bad day
BOBO	5. A baboon
LONELY	6. These people need visitors
ATTACK	7. Mr. Pignati had a heart ___
PEANUTS	8. Food for Bobo
ALBERT	9. The prince in a can
WALL	10. Street where Kenneth works
TONY	11. ___'s market; sells beer to anyone
LATIN	12. Club Lorraine used as an excuse for not being home
CONCHETTA	13. Mrs. Pignati. She's not in California.
CHECK	14. Mr. Pignati gave the L&J fund one for $10
LOVER	15. Sex
FUND	16. The L & J ___
ELECTRICIAN	17. Mr. Pignati's former occupation
HUSBAND	18. Love
PEACOCK	19. Lorraine was attacked by a low IQ ___
PIGMAN	20. Mr. Pignati

The Pigman Fill In The Blanks 3

_____

1. What Mr. Pignati buys J & L to eat
2. _____ marathon
3. Mr. Pignati had a heart ___
4. John's older brother
5. The ___; John's father
6. Love
7. Money
8. Mr. Pignati's first name
9. Sex
10. Magic
11. Peanut lady, peacock, & nocturnal room were ___ of a bad day
12. Food for Bobo
13. The librarian
14. The L & J ___
15. Dennis's last name
16. Supercolossal fruit ____
17. Roller rink activity at Mr Pignati's house
18. These people need visitors
19. 'Old maid' English teacher
20. Avenue; Mr. Pignati's street

The Pigman Fill In The Blanks 3 Answer Key

DELICACIES	1. What Mr. Pignati buys J & L to eat
TELEPHONE	2. _____ marathon
ATTACK	3. Mr. Pignati had a heart ___
KENNETH	4. John's older brother
BORE	5. The ___; John's father
HUSBAND	6. Love
ASSASSIN	7. Money
ANGELO	8. Mr. Pignati's first name
LOVER	9. Sex
BOATMAN	10. Magic
OMENS	11. Peanut lady, peacock, & nocturnal room were ___ of a bad day
PEANUTS	12. Food for Bobo
CRICKET	13. The librarian
FUND	14. The L & J ___
KOBIN	15. Dennis's last name
ROLL	16. Supercolossal fruit ____
SKATING	17. Roller rink activity at Mr Pignati's house
LONELY	18. These people need visitors
KING	19. 'Old maid' English teacher
HOWARD	20. Avenue; Mr. Pignati's street

The Pigman Fill In The Blanks 4

_____
_____
_____
_____
_____
_____
_____
_____
_____
_____
_____
_____
_____
_____
_____
_____
_____
_____
_____
_____

1. ____ Kid; Norton

2. The ___; John's father

3. Sex

4. Dear ___

5. The prince in a can

6. Mr. Pignati's former occupation

7. Magic

8. Mr. Pignati's first name

9. ___'s market; sells beer to anyone

10. Club Lorraine used as an excuse for not being home

11. A baboon

12. What Mr. Pignati buys J & L to eat

13. She fixed the attendance cards for L & J

14. Street where Kenneth works

15. Mr. Pignati gave the L&J fund one for $10

16. Bobo's home

17. School friend of John & Lorraine

18. Roller rink activity at Mr Pignati's house

19. Mrs. Pignati. She's not in California.

20. The librarian

The Pigman Fill In The Blanks 4 Answer Key

MARSHMALLOW	1.	____ Kid; Norton
BORE	2.	The ___; John's father
LOVER	3.	Sex
ALICE	4.	Dear ___
ALBERT	5.	The prince in a can
ELECTRICIAN	6.	Mr. Pignati's former occupation
BOATMAN	7.	Magic
ANGELO	8.	Mr. Pignati's first name
TONY	9.	___'s market; sells beer to anyone
LATIN	10.	Club Lorraine used as an excuse for not being home
BOBO	11.	A baboon
DELICACIES	12.	What Mr. Pignati buys J & L to eat
DEANNA	13.	She fixed the attendance cards for L & J
WALL	14.	Street where Kenneth works
CHECK	15.	Mr. Pignati gave the L&J fund one for $10
ZOO	16.	Bobo's home
DENNIS	17.	School friend of John & Lorraine
SKATING	18.	Roller rink activity at Mr Pignati's house
CONCHETTA	19.	Mrs. Pignati. She's not in California.
CRICKET	20.	The librarian

The Pigman Matching 1

___ 1. PEACOCK   A. Dear ___
___ 2. HOWARD   B. ____ Kid; Norton
___ 3. BORE   C. Masterson's ____
___ 4. OLD   D. ____ Park Zoo
___ 5. PIGS   E. Mr. Pignati
___ 6. LONELY   F. What Mr. Pignati buys J & L to eat
___ 7. ALICE   G. Roller rink activity at Mr Pignati's house
___ 8. PIGMAN   H. She fixed the attendance cards for L & J
___ 9. MARSHMALLOW   I. 'Old maid' English teacher
___ 10. BARON   J. Mr. Pignati's first name
___ 11. CONCHETTA   K. ____ marathon
___ 12. ODDBALL   L. Love
___ 13. FUND   M. Money
___ 14. TOMB   N. The L & J ___
___ 15. ANGELO   O. ... get your hair cut. You look like an ___.
___ 16. ELECTRICIAN   P. The ___; John's father
___ 17. HUSBAND   Q. What Mr. Pignati collects
___ 18. WALL   R. Avenue; Mr. Pignati's street
___ 19. TELEPHONE   S. John's mother: ___ Lady
___ 20. KING   T. Mrs. Pignati. She's not in California.
___ 21. SKATING   U. These people need visitors
___ 22. CRICKET   V. Lorraine was attacked by a low IQ ___
___ 23. DEANNA   W. Mr. Pignati's former occupation
___ 24. ASSASSIN   X. Street where Kenneth works
___ 25. DELICACIES   Y. The librarian

The Pigman Matching 1 Answer Key

V - 1. PEACOCK	A. Dear ___
R - 2. HOWARD	B. ___ Kid; Norton
P - 3. BORE	C. Masterson's ___
S - 4. OLD	D. ___ Park Zoo
Q - 5. PIGS	E. Mr. Pignati
U - 6. LONELY	F. What Mr. Pignati buys J & L to eat
A - 7. ALICE	G. Roller rink activity at Mr Pignati's house
E - 8. PIGMAN	H. She fixed the attendance cards for L & J
B - 9. MARSHMALLOW	I. 'Old maid' English teacher
D - 10. BARON	J. Mr. Pignati's first name
T - 11. CONCHETTA	K. ___ marathon
O - 12. ODDBALL	L. Love
N - 13. FUND	M. Money
C - 14. TOMB	N. The L & J ___
J - 15. ANGELO	O. ... get your hair cut. You look like an ___.
W - 16. ELECTRICIAN	P. The ___; John's father
L - 17. HUSBAND	Q. What Mr. Pignati collects
X - 18. WALL	R. Avenue; Mr. Pignati's street
K - 19. TELEPHONE	S. John's mother: ___ Lady
I - 20. KING	T. Mrs. Pignati. She's not in California.
G - 21. SKATING	U. These people need visitors
Y - 22. CRICKET	V. Lorraine was attacked by a low IQ ___
H - 23. DEANNA	W. Mr. Pignati's former occupation
M - 24. ASSASSIN	X. Street where Kenneth works
F - 25. DELICACIES	Y. The librarian

The Pigman Matching 2

___ 1. CONCHETTA
___ 2. FUND
___ 3. DELICACIES
___ 4. ZOO
___ 5. PIGS
___ 6. KENNETH
___ 7. ALBERT
___ 8. HUSBAND
___ 9. CHECK
___ 10. LOVER
___ 11. AHRA
___ 12. ALICE
___ 13. LONELY
___ 14. DENNIS
___ 15. NORTON
___ 16. BOMBER
___ 17. OMENS
___ 18. BARON
___ 19. ELECTRICIAN
___ 20. OLD
___ 21. LATIN
___ 22. DEANNA
___ 23. ASSASSIN
___ 24. HOWARD
___ 25. ROLL

A. John's mother: ___ Lady
B. What Mr. Pignati collects
C. She fixed the attendance cards for L & J
D. Love
E. Peanut lady, peacock, & nocturnal room were ___ of a bad day
F. The L & J ___
G. What Mr. Pignati buys J & L to eat
H. School friend of John & Lorraine
I. Has a habit of shoplifting
J. The prince in a can
K. Mr. Pignati gave the L&J fund one for $10
L. These people need visitors
M. Money
N. John's older brother
O. ___ Park Zoo
P. Mrs. Pignati. She's not in California.
Q. Avenue; Mr. Pignati's street
R. Dear ___
S. Aunt whose ghost gets blamed
T. Sex
U. Bobo's home
V. Club Lorraine used as an excuse for not being home
W. Supercolossal fruit ___
X. Mr. Pignati's former occupation
Y. Bathroom ___

The Pigman Matching 2 Answer Key

P - 1. CONCHETTA   A. John's mother: ___ Lady
F - 2. FUND   B. What Mr. Pignati collects
G - 3. DELICACIES   C. She fixed the attendance cards for L & J
U - 4. ZOO   D. Love
B - 5. PIGS   E. Peanut lady, peacock, & nocturnal room were ___ of a bad day
N - 6. KENNETH   F. The L & J ___
J - 7. ALBERT   G. What Mr. Pignati buys J & L to eat
D - 8. HUSBAND   H. School friend of John & Lorraine
K - 9. CHECK   I. Has a habit of shoplifting
T - 10. LOVER   J. The prince in a can
S - 11. AHRA   K. Mr. Pignati gave the L&J fund one for $10
R - 12. ALICE   L. These people need visitors
L - 13. LONELY   M. Money
H - 14. DENNIS   N. John's older brother
I - 15. NORTON   O. ___ Park Zoo
Y - 16. BOMBER   P. Mrs. Pignati. She's not in California.
E - 17. OMENS   Q. Avenue; Mr. Pignati's street
O - 18. BARON   R. Dear ___
X - 19. ELECTRICIAN   S. Aunt whose ghost gets blamed
A - 20. OLD   T. Sex
V - 21. LATIN   U. Bobo's home
C - 22. DEANNA   V. Club Lorraine used as an excuse for not being home
M - 23. ASSASSIN   W. Supercolossal fruit ___
Q - 24. HOWARD   X. Mr. Pignati's former occupation
W - 25. ROLL   Y. Bathroom ___

The Pigman Matching 3

___ 1. LONELY   A. Dear ___
___ 2. ROLL   B. ... get your hair cut. You look like an ___.
___ 3. FUND   C. John's older brother
___ 4. DEANNA   D. She fixed the attendance cards for L & J
___ 5. ASSASSIN   E. Mr. Pignati's first name
___ 6. CHECK   F. ___ Park Zoo
___ 7. OMENS   G. John's mother: ___ Lady
___ 8. ANGELO   H. Has a habit of shoplifting
___ 9. PIGMAN   I. 'Old maid' English teacher
___ 10. NORTON   J. Magic
___ 11. TOMB   K. The L & J ___
___ 12. ZOO   L. Money
___ 13. TONY   M. These people need visitors
___ 14. TELEPHONE   N. The librarian
___ 15. BARON   O. ___'s market; sells beer to anyone
___ 16. CRICKET   P. Mr. Pignati gave the L&J fund one for $10
___ 17. PIGS   Q. Mr. Pignati
___ 18. ODDBALL   R. Peanut lady, peacock, & nocturnal room were ___ of a bad day
___ 19. ATTACK   S. Bobo's home
___ 20. KENNETH   T. ___ marathon
___ 21. OLD   U. Mr. Pignati had a heart ___
___ 22. PEANUTS   V. Supercolossal fruit ___
___ 23. BOATMAN   W. Masterson's ___
___ 24. KING   X. Food for Bobo
___ 25. ALICE   Y. What Mr. Pignati collects

The Pigman Matching 3 Answer Key

M - 1. LONELY
V - 2. ROLL
K - 3. FUND
D - 4. DEANNA
L - 5. ASSASSIN
P - 6. CHECK
R - 7. OMENS
E - 8. ANGELO
Q - 9. PIGMAN
H - 10. NORTON
W - 11. TOMB
S - 12. ZOO
O - 13. TONY
T - 14. TELEPHONE
F - 15. BARON
N - 16. CRICKET
Y - 17. PIGS
B - 18. ODDBALL
U - 19. ATTACK
C - 20. KENNETH
G - 21. OLD
X - 22. PEANUTS
J - 23. BOATMAN
I - 24. KING
A - 25. ALICE

A. Dear ___
B. ... get your hair cut. You look like an ___.
C. John's older brother
D. She fixed the attendance cards for L & J
E. Mr. Pignati's first name
F. ___ Park Zoo
G. John's mother: ___ Lady
H. Has a habit of shoplifting
I. 'Old maid' English teacher
J. Magic
K. The L & J ___
L. Money
M. These people need visitors
N. The librarian
O. ___'s market; sells beer to anyone
P. Mr. Pignati gave the L&J fund one for $10
Q. Mr. Pignati
R. Peanut lady, peacock, & nocturnal room were ___ of a bad day
S. Bobo's home
T. ___ marathon
U. Mr. Pignati had a heart ___
V. Supercolossal fruit ___
W. Masterson's ___
X. Food for Bobo
Y. What Mr. Pignati collects

The Pigman Matching 4

___ 1. KING
___ 2. LATIN
___ 3. BORE
___ 4. TONY
___ 5. BOBO
___ 6. LOVER
___ 7. PIGS
___ 8. ROLL
___ 9. AHRA
___ 10. DELICACIES
___ 11. ELECTRICIAN
___ 12. ATTACK
___ 13. ASSASSIN
___ 14. NORTON
___ 15. KENNETH
___ 16. HUSBAND
___ 17. ANGELO
___ 18. KOBIN
___ 19. ALICE
___ 20. PEACOCK
___ 21. OMENS
___ 22. CONCHETTA
___ 23. ODDBALL
___ 24. TOMB
___ 25. BOMBER

A. What Mr. Pignati collects
B. Sex
C. Mr. Pignati's former occupation
D. Love
E. Money
F. ___'s market; sells beer to anyone
G. Bathroom ___
H. Aunt whose ghost gets blamed
I. Supercolossal fruit ___
J. Peanut lady, peacock, & nocturnal room were ___ of a bad day
K. The ___; John's father
L. ... get your hair cut. You look like an ___.
M. Has a habit of shoplifting
N. 'Old maid' English teacher
O. What Mr. Pignati buys J & L to eat
P. Mrs. Pignati. She's not in California.
Q. Masterson's ___
R. Lorraine was attacked by a low IQ ___
S. Club Lorraine used as an excuse for not being home
T. Dear ___
U. Dennis's last name
V. A baboon
W. Mr. Pignati's first name
X. John's older brother
Y. Mr. Pignati had a heart ___

The Pigman Matching 4 Answer Key

N - 1. KING	A. What Mr. Pignati collects
S - 2. LATIN	B. Sex
K - 3. BORE	C. Mr. Pignati's former occupation
F - 4. TONY	D. Love
V - 5. BOBO	E. Money
B - 6. LOVER	F. ___'s market; sells beer to anyone
A - 7. PIGS	G. Bathroom ___
I - 8. ROLL	H. Aunt whose ghost gets blamed
H - 9. AHRA	I. Supercolossal fruit ___
O - 10. DELICACIES	J. Peanut lady, peacock, & nocturnal room were ___ of a bad day
C - 11. ELECTRICIAN	K. The ___; John's father
Y - 12. ATTACK	L. ... get your hair cut. You look like an ___.
E - 13. ASSASSIN	M. Has a habit of shoplifting
M - 14. NORTON	N. 'Old maid' English teacher
X - 15. KENNETH	O. What Mr. Pignati buys J & L to eat
D - 16. HUSBAND	P. Mrs. Pignati. She's not in California.
W - 17. ANGELO	Q. Masterson's ___
U - 18. KOBIN	R. Lorraine was attacked by a low IQ ___
T - 19. ALICE	S. Club Lorraine used as an excuse for not being home
R - 20. PEACOCK	T. Dear ___
J - 21. OMENS	U. Dennis's last name
P - 22. CONCHETTA	V. A baboon
L - 23. ODDBALL	W. Mr. Pignati's first name
Q - 24. TOMB	X. John's older brother
G - 25. BOMBER	Y. Mr. Pignati had a heart ___

The Pigman Magic Squares 1

Match the definition with the vocabulary word. Put your answers in the magic squares below. When your answers are correct, all columns and rows will add to the same number.

A. WALL
B. SKATING
C. BORE
D. TELEPHONE
E. ROLL
F. LONELY
G. NORTON
H. ATTACK
I. ELECTRICIAN
J. CHECK
K. BOATMAN
L. PIGMAN
M. ODDBALL
N. ALICE
O. LOVER
P. TONY

1. Sex
2. _____ marathon
3. Mr. Pignati gave the L&J fund one for $10
4. Supercolossal fruit _____
5. Mr. Pignati's former occupation
6. These people need visitors
7. ___'s market; sells beer to anyone
8. The ___; John's father
9. Mr. Pignati had a heart ___
10. Magic
11. Street where Kenneth works
12. Dear ___
13. Roller rink activity at Mr Pignati's house
14. ... get your hair cut. You look like an ___.
15. Has a habit of shoplifting
16. Mr. Pignati

A=	B=	C=	D=
E=	F=	G=	H=
I=	J=	K=	L=
M=	N=	O=	P=

The Pigman Magic Squares 1 Answer Key

Match the definition with the vocabulary word. Put your answers in the magic squares below. When your answers are correct, all columns and rows will add to the same number.

A. WALL
B. SKATING
C. BORE
D. TELEPHONE
E. ROLL
F. LONELY
G. NORTON
H. ATTACK
I. ELECTRICIAN
J. CHECK
K. BOATMAN
L. PIGMAN
M. ODDBALL
N. ALICE
O. LOVER
P. TONY

1. Sex
2. _____ marathon
3. Mr. Pignati gave the L&J fund one for $10
4. Supercolossal fruit ____
5. Mr. Pignati's former occupation
6. These people need visitors
7. ___'s market; sells beer to anyone
8. The ___; John's father
9. Mr. Pignati had a heart ___
10. Magic
11. Street where Kenneth works
12. Dear ___
13. Roller rink activity at Mr Pignati's house
14. ... get your hair cut. You look like an ___.
15. Has a habit of shoplifting
16. Mr. Pignati

A=11	B=13	C=8	D=2
E=4	F=6	G=15	H=9
I=5	J=3	K=10	L=16
M=14	N=12	O=1	P=7

The Pigman Magic Squares 2

Match the definition with the vocabulary word. Put your answers in the magic squares below. When your answers are correct, all columns and rows will add to the same number.

A. BARON
B. WIFE
C. HOWARD
D. LOVER
E. LONELY
F. ALBERT
G. ATTACK
H. LATIN
I. KOBIN
J. NORTON
K. CONCHETTA
L. DELICACIES
M. BOATMAN
N. OLD
O. TOMB
P. ASSASSIN

1. Club Lorraine used as an excuse for not being home
2. ____ Park Zoo
3. Fun
4. Mr. Pignati had a heart ____
5. Has a habit of shoplifting
6. Masterson's ____
7. Money
8. Dennis's last name
9. Mrs. Pignati. She's not in California.
10. John's mother: ____ Lady
11. Magic
12. What Mr. Pignati buys J & L to eat
13. These people need visitors
14. Sex
15. Avenue; Mr. Pignati's street
16. The prince in a can

A=	B=	C=	D=
E=	F=	G=	H=
I=	J=	K=	L=
M=	N=	O=	P=

The Pigman Magic Squares 2 Answer Key

Match the definition with the vocabulary word. Put your answers in the magic squares below. When your answers are correct, all columns and rows will add to the same number.

A. BARON
B. WIFE
C. HOWARD
D. LOVER
E. LONELY
F. ALBERT
G. ATTACK
H. LATIN
I. KOBIN
J. NORTON
K. CONCHETTA
L. DELICACIES
M. BOATMAN
N. OLD
O. TOMB
P. ASSASSIN

1. Club Lorraine used as an excuse for not being home
2. ____ Park Zoo
3. Fun
4. Mr. Pignati had a heart ___
5. Has a habit of shoplifting
6. Masterson's ____
7. Money
8. Dennis's last name
9. Mrs. Pignati. She's not in California.
10. John's mother: ___ Lady
11. Magic
12. What Mr. Pignati buys J & L to eat
13. These people need visitors
14. Sex
15. Avenue; Mr. Pignati's street
16. The prince in a can

A=2	B=3	C=15	D=14
E=13	F=16	G=4	H=1
I=8	J=5	K=9	L=12
M=11	N=10	O=6	P=7

The Pigman Magic Squares 3

Match the definition with the vocabulary word. Put your answers in the magic squares below. When your answers are correct, all columns and rows will add to the same number.

A. BOMBER
B. BORE
C. TONY
D. HOWARD
E. WALL
F. PIGMAN
G. BOATMAN
H. ELECTRICIAN
I. OMENS
J. DENNIS
K. LONELY
L. ODDBALL
M. ATTACK
N. WIFE
O. DELICACIES
P. KOBIN

1. Fun
2. Magic
3. ... get your hair cut. You look like an ___.
4. Bathroom ___
5. These people need visitors
6. The ___; John's father
7. Mr. Pignati had a heart ___
8. Mr. Pignati's former occupation
9. Street where Kenneth works
10. Dennis's last name
11. ___'s market; sells beer to anyone
12. School friend of John & Lorraine
13. Avenue; Mr. Pignati's street
14. Peanut lady, peacock, & nocturnal room were ___ of a bad day
15. Mr. Pignati
16. What Mr. Pignati buys J & L to eat

A=	B=	C=	D=
E=	F=	G=	H=
I=	J=	K=	L=
M=	N=	O=	P=

The Pigman Magic Squares 3 Answer Key

Match the definition with the vocabulary word. Put your answers in the magic squares below. When your answers are correct, all columns and rows will add to the same number.

A. BOMBER
B. BORE
C. TONY
D. HOWARD
E. WALL
F. PIGMAN
G. BOATMAN
H. ELECTRICIAN
I. OMENS
J. DENNIS
K. LONELY
L. ODDBALL
M. ATTACK
N. WIFE
O. DELICACIES
P. KOBIN

1. Fun
2. Magic
3. ... get your hair cut. You look like an ___.
4. Bathroom ___
5. These people need visitors
6. The ___; John's father
7. Mr. Pignati had a heart ___
8. Mr. Pignati's former occupation
9. Street where Kenneth works
10. Dennis's last name
11. ___'s market; sells beer to anyone
12. School friend of John & Lorraine
13. Avenue; Mr. Pignati's street
14. Peanut lady, peacock, & nocturnal room were ___ of a bad day
15. Mr. Pignati
16. What Mr. Pignati buys J & L to eat

A=4	B=6	C=11	D=13
E=9	F=15	G=2	H=8
I=14	J=12	K=5	L=3
M=7	N=1	O=16	P=10

The Pigman Magic Squares 4

Match the definition with the vocabulary word. Put your answers in the magic squares below. When your answers are correct, all columns and rows will add to the same number.

A. CRICKET
B. NORTON
C. LONELY
D. ODDBALL
E. ASSASSIN
F. PEACOCK
G. KENNETH
H. ZOO
I. SKATING
J. CONCHETTA
K. ELECTRICIAN
L. KOBIN
M. BOBO
N. BARON
O. TELEPHONE
P. ALICE

1. Has a habit of shoplifting
2. John's older brother
3. Mr. Pignati's former occupation
4. ____ Park Zoo
5. A baboon
6. Dennis's last name
7. Bobo's home
8. The librarian
9. Dear ___
10. Roller rink activity at Mr Pignati's house
11. Money
12. ... get your hair cut. You look like an ___.
13. These people need visitors
14. Lorraine was attacked by a low IQ ___
15. Mrs. Pignati. She's not in California.
16. _____ marathon

A=	B=	C=	D=
E=	F=	G=	H=
I=	J=	K=	L=
M=	N=	O=	P=

The Pigman Magic Squares 4 Answer Key

Match the definition with the vocabulary word. Put your answers in the magic squares below. When your answers are correct, all columns and rows will add to the same number.

A. CRICKET
B. NORTON
C. LONELY
D. ODDBALL
E. ASSASSIN
F. PEACOCK
G. KENNETH
H. ZOO
I. SKATING
J. CONCHETTA
K. ELECTRICIAN
L. KOBIN
M. BOBO
N. BARON
O. TELEPHONE
P. ALICE

1. Has a habit of shoplifting
2. John's older brother
3. Mr. Pignati's former occupation
4. ____ Park Zoo
5. A baboon
6. Dennis's last name
7. Bobo's home
8. The librarian
9. Dear ___
10. Roller rink activity at Mr Pignati's house
11. Money
12. ... get your hair cut. You look like an ___.
13. These people need visitors
14. Lorraine was attacked by a low IQ ___
15. Mrs. Pignati. She's not in California.
16. _____ marathon

A=8	B=1	C=13	D=12
E=11	F=14	G=2	H=7
I=10	J=15	K=3	L=6
M=5	N=4	O=16	P=9

The Pigman Word Search 1

Words are placed backwards, forward, diagonally, up and down. Clues listed below can help you find the words. Circle the hidden vocabulary words in the maze.

```
L V B K K V Y D K K Z A R C A T T B
S G I P T E L E P H O N E O H R Y R
D K S W N R E A B K Y G B D R E R Y
G V A O Z W N N T O C E M D A B C H
V N R T Y P O N N I B L O B Y L L K
N A M G I P L A O Z N O B A W A L L
B I S S B N V H R B G L Q L W O O X
H C P S O W G J T J T D Q L V Q R F
O I E W A C Y N O T O M B E R O B S
W R A I T S B G N O V P R V Y N C X
A T C F M S S N Z N R E J W P N R T
R C O E A A L I C E B A P Z S D I H
D E C N N K S K N K T N M Y N N C J
J L K M W I O C C T B U Q A E U K Y
B E T Q N S T B A B R T B V M F E W
K E N N E T H C I L X S P D O T T J
Y N E T M R K Y F N U G V N R Y Q V
B D Z P F C O N C H E T T A D P B P
```

'Old maid' English teacher (4)
... get your hair cut. You look like an ___. (7)
A baboon (4)
Aunt whose ghost gets blamed (4)
Avenue; Mr. Pignati's street (6)
Bathroom ____ (6)
Bobo's home (3)
Club Lorraine used as an excuse for not being home (5)
Dear ___ (5)
Dennis's last name (5)
Food for Bobo (7)
Fun (4)
Has a habit of shoplifting (6)
John's mother: ___ Lady (3)
John's older brother (7)
Lorraine was attacked by a low IQ ___ (7)
Love (7)
Magic (7)
Masterson's ____ (4)
Money (8)
Mr. Pignati (6)

Mr. Pignati gave the L&J fund one for $10 (5)
Mr. Pignati had a heart ___ (6)
Mr. Pignati's first name (6)
Mr. Pignati's former occupation (11)
Mrs. Pignati. She's not in California. (9)
Peanut lady, peacock, & nocturnal room were ___ of a bad day (5)
Roller rink activity at Mr Pignati's house (7)
School friend of John & Lorraine (6)
Sex (5)
She fixed the attendance cards for L & J (6)
Street where Kenneth works (4)
Supercolossal fruit ____ (4)
The L & J ___ (4)
The ___; John's father (4)
The librarian (7)
The prince in a can (6)
These people need visitors (6)
What Mr. Pignati collects (4)
___'s market; sells beer to anyone (4)
____ Park Zoo (5)
_____ marathon (9)

The Pigman Word Search 1 Answer Key

Words are placed backwards, forward, diagonally, up and down. Clues listed below can help you find the words. Circle the hidden vocabulary words in the maze.

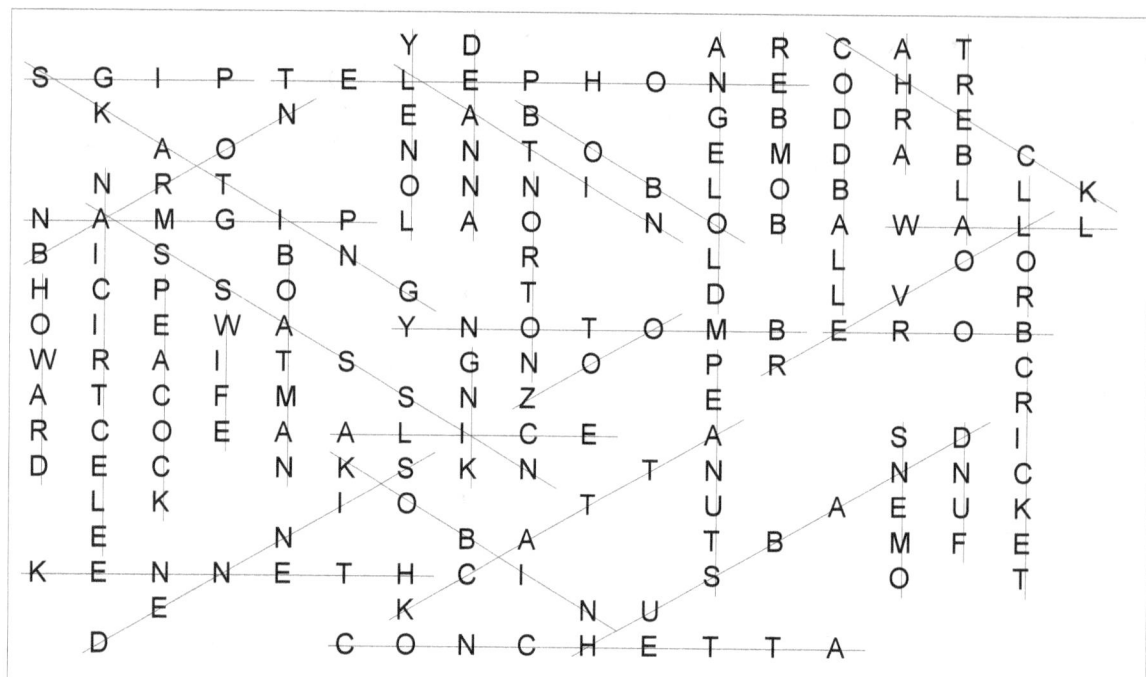

'Old maid' English teacher (4)
... get your hair cut. You look like an ___. (7)
A baboon (4)
Aunt whose ghost gets blamed (4)
Avenue; Mr. Pignati's street (6)
Bathroom ____ (6)
Bobo's home (3)
Club Lorraine used as an excuse for not being home (5)
Dear ___ (5)
Dennis's last name (5)
Food for Bobo (7)
Fun (4)
Has a habit of shoplifting (6)
John's mother: ___ Lady (3)
John's older brother (7)
Lorraine was attacked by a low IQ ___ (7)
Love (7)
Magic (7)
Masterson's ____ (4)
Money (8)
Mr. Pignati (6)

Mr. Pignati gave the L&J fund one for $10 (5)
Mr. Pignati had a heart ___ (6)
Mr. Pignati's first name (6)
Mr. Pignati's former occupation (11)
Mrs. Pignati. She's not in California. (9)
Peanut lady, peacock, & nocturnal room were ___ of a bad day (5)
Roller rink activity at Mr Pignati's house (7)
School friend of John & Lorraine (6)
Sex (5)
She fixed the attendance cards for L & J (6)
Street where Kenneth works (4)
Supercolossal fruit ____ (4)
The L & J ___ (4)
The ___; John's father (4)
The librarian (7)
The prince in a can (6)
These people need visitors (6)
What Mr. Pignati collects (4)
___'s market; sells beer to anyone (4)
____ Park Zoo (5)
_____ marathon (9)

The Pigman Word Search 2

Words are placed backwards, forward, diagonally, up and down. Clues listed below can help you find the words. Circle the hidden vocabulary words in the maze.

```
D E A N N A L N S A Q S K A T I N G
S X P T Z C I O P N K G E Z P K E G
C H E C K T N C V G W I N Y G G N R
P V B P A B O M B E R X N O R T O N
T E S L H Y G H C L R O E G L L H Y
P E A N U T S I C O T N T W L D P H
H C O C T Z L R L N R M H W P D E D
W O L D O A I B X G W B O R E P L H
Z N W L T C K K O O Z S N W I T E T
A C W A K L K Y L A H N I G A N T E
L H P E R S D L D W T E S K L L F J
B E T I H D A E E B F M S L O I L K
E T O H G M M N O U O A V W B Q T
R T M M H M G O N B N B S N W G I P
T A B S Y J A L I O D B S O J D V N
K L R K R V Q N S D X V A R M B Q G
M A B W P P P J O H U S B A N D X V
M A T T A C K J V F J M R B A H R A
```

'Old maid' English teacher (4)
... get your hair cut. You look like an ___. (7)
A baboon (4)
Aunt whose ghost gets blamed (4)
Avenue; Mr. Pignati's street (6)
Bathroom ___ (6)
Bobo's home (3)
Club Lorraine used as an excuse for not being home (5)
Dear ___ (5)
Dennis's last name (5)
Food for Bobo (7)
Fun (4)
Has a habit of shoplifting (6)
John's mother: ___ Lady (3)
John's older brother (7)
Lorraine was attacked by a low IQ ___ (7)
Love (7)
Magic (7)
Masterson's ___ (4)
Money (8)
Mr. Pignati (6)

Mr. Pignati gave the L&J fund one for $10 (5)
Mr. Pignati had a heart ___ (6)
Mr. Pignati's first name (6)
Mrs. Pignati. She's not in California. (9)
Peanut lady, peacock, & nocturnal room were ___ of a bad day (5)
Roller rink activity at Mr Pignati's house (7)
School friend of John & Lorraine (6)
Sex (5)
She fixed the attendance cards for L & J (6)
Street where Kenneth works (4)
Supercolossal fruit ___ (4)
The L & J ___ (4)
The ___; John's father (4)
The librarian (7)
The prince in a can (6)
These people need visitors (6)
What Mr. Pignati collects (4)
___'s market; sells beer to anyone (4)
___ Kid; Norton (11)
___ Park Zoo (5)
___ marathon (9)

The Pigman Word Search 2 Answer Key

Words are placed backwards, forward, diagonally, up and down. Clues listed below can help you find the words. Circle the hidden vocabulary words in the maze.

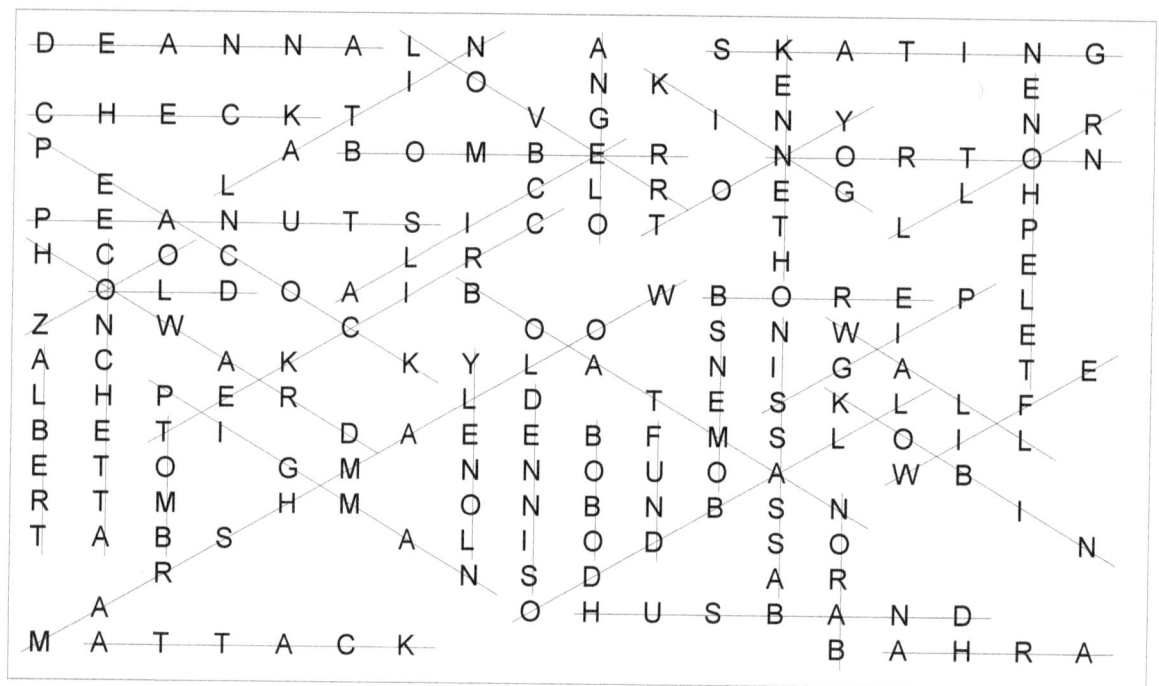

'Old maid' English teacher (4)
... get your hair cut. You look like an ___. (7)
A baboon (4)
Aunt whose ghost gets blamed (4)
Avenue; Mr. Pignati's street (6)
Bathroom ____ (6)
Bobo's home (3)
Club Lorraine used as an excuse for not being home (5)
Dear ___ (5)
Dennis's last name (5)
Food for Bobo (7)
Fun (4)
Has a habit of shoplifting (6)
John's mother: ___ Lady (3)
John's older brother (7)
Lorraine was attacked by a low IQ ___ (7)
Love (7)
Magic (7)
Masterson's ____ (4)
Money (8)
Mr. Pignati (6)

Mr. Pignati gave the L&J fund one for $10 (5)
Mr. Pignati had a heart ___ (6)
Mr. Pignati's first name (6)
Mrs. Pignati. She's not in California. (9)
Peanut lady, peacock, & nocturnal room were ___ of a bad day (5)
Roller rink activity at Mr Pignati's house (7)
School friend of John & Lorraine (6)
Sex (5)
She fixed the attendance cards for L & J (6)
Street where Kenneth works (4)
Supercolossal fruit ____ (4)
The L & J ___ (4)
The ___; John's father (4)
The librarian (7)
The prince in a can (6)
These people need visitors (6)
What Mr. Pignati collects (4)
___'s market; sells beer to anyone (4)
____ Kid; Norton (11)
____ Park Zoo (5)
_____ marathon (9)

The Pigman Word Search 3

Words are placed backwards, forward, diagonally, up and down. Words listed below are included in the maze. Circle the hidden vocabulary words in the maze.

```
T K H B K K C E H C P S G I P N P F
E O O M E O X L X O E T K T E O F Y
L R N L N G B H M I W H Y O A R U M
E T V Y N W G I C D Q A T M N T N F
P K J O E T I A N N E S R B U O D K
H B R L T X C F P A L N K D T N R T
O C O D H I V Z E B E E N Q S E N N
N O L B L Z J T A S C M M I B S A P
E N L E O O J R C U T O F M S M M H
Y C D V Z O H S O H R D O Y T Y G G
H H W J O A V S C R I B F A O Z I J
W E D S D T T K K N C G O L N H P P
G T Q L D L D A L E I B E D Q N T Q
X T L L B E Q T C O A G S G O R C N
B A S S A S S I N G N I K R E V O L
W T H N L T L N C A V E A B H P M K
Y W N J L A I G K W M B L K G M R S
Q A T T A C K N K F F A K Y P G M P
```

AHRA	CHECK	KOBIN	PIGS
ALBERT	CONCHETTA	LATIN	ROLL
ALICE	DEANNA	LONELY	SKATING
ANGELO	DELICACIES	LOVER	TELEPHONE
ASSASSIN	DENNIS	NORTON	TOMB
ATTACK	ELECTRICIAN	ODDBALL	TONY
BARON	FUND	OLD	WALL
BOATMAN	HOWARD	OMENS	WIFE
BOBO	HUSBAND	PEACOCK	ZOO
BOMBER	KENNETH	PEANUTS	
BORE	KING	PIGMAN	

The Pigman Word Search 3 Answer Key

Words are placed backwards, forward, diagonally, up and down. Words listed below are included in the maze. Circle the hidden vocabulary words in the maze.

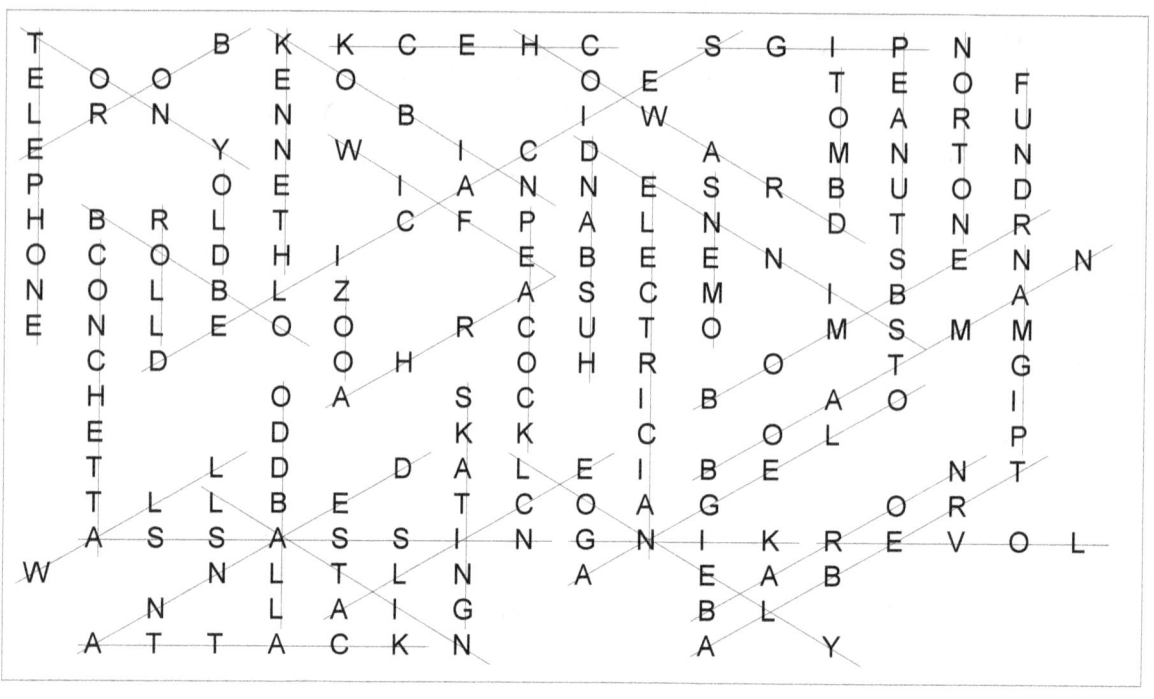

AHRA	CHECK	KOBIN	PIGS
ALBERT	CONCHETTA	LATIN	ROLL
ALICE	DEANNA	LONELY	SKATING
ANGELO	DELICACIES	LOVER	TELEPHONE
ASSASSIN	DENNIS	NORTON	TOMB
ATTACK	ELECTRICIAN	ODDBALL	TONY
BARON	FUND	OLD	WALL
BOATMAN	HOWARD	OMENS	WIFE
BOBO	HUSBAND	PEACOCK	ZOO
BOMBER	KENNETH	PEANUTS	
BORE	KING	PIGMAN	

The Pigman Word Search 4

Words are placed backwards, forward, diagonally, up and down. Words listed below are included in the maze. Circle the hidden vocabulary words in the maze.

M	C	V	L	C	H	E	C	K	L	L	A	B	D	D	O	P	Y
A	A	Z	H	O	N	W	E	S	O	A	L	Y	W	E	J	E	P
H	W	R	M	Z	N	T	C	D	V	T	R	J	D	L	G	A	N
R	V	E	S	P	F	E	I	G	E	I	B	N	C	I	F	C	R
A	N	Q	D	H	H	Z	L	P	R	N	A	B	W	C	T	O	T
S	G	W	F	D	M	L	A	Y	E	B	R	O	F	A	G	C	R
H	N	N	R	T	O	A	K	T	S	A	O	B	K	C	L	K	S
A	L	B	E	R	T	G	L	U	W	F	N	O	S	I	P	L	S
W	A	M	B	D	T	V	H	L	Y	X	B	U	Z	E	I	B	J
T	S	C	M	Z	F	B	L	S	O	I	S	X	T	S	G	H	B
S	S	K	O	N	M	B	O	K	N	W	B	N	B	S	M	T	H
B	A	E	B	V	C	F	S	A	Q	P	R	N	C	D	A	D	W
Z	S	N	K	W	K	D	C	T	T	B	Q	D	O	V	N	R	T
Y	S	N	C	C	I	I	E	I	G	M	Q	E	M	R	Q	A	W
C	I	E	A	T	Z	F	N	N	S	O	A	A	D	L	T	W	S
Q	N	T	O	N	Y	K	E	G	N	T	A	N	G	E	L	O	C
Y	T	H	T	E	K	C	I	R	C	I	U	N	Y	Q	O	H	N
A	B	O	R	E	G	P	O	L	D	F	S	A	X	Z	Y	D	F

AHRA	DELICACIES	OLD
ALBERT	DENNIS	OMENS
ALICE	FUND	PEACOCK
ANGELO	HOWARD	PEANUTS
ASSASSIN	HUSBAND	PIGMAN
ATTACK	KENNETH	PIGS
BARON	KING	ROLL
BOATMAN	KOBIN	SKATING
BOBO	LATIN	TOMB
BOMBER	LONELY	TONY
BORE	LOVER	WALL
CHECK	MARSHMALLOW	WIFE
CRICKET	NORTON	ZOO
DEANNA	ODDBALL	

The Pigman Word Search 4 Answer Key

Words are placed backwards, forward, diagonally, up and down. Words listed below are included in the maze. Circle the hidden vocabulary words in the maze.

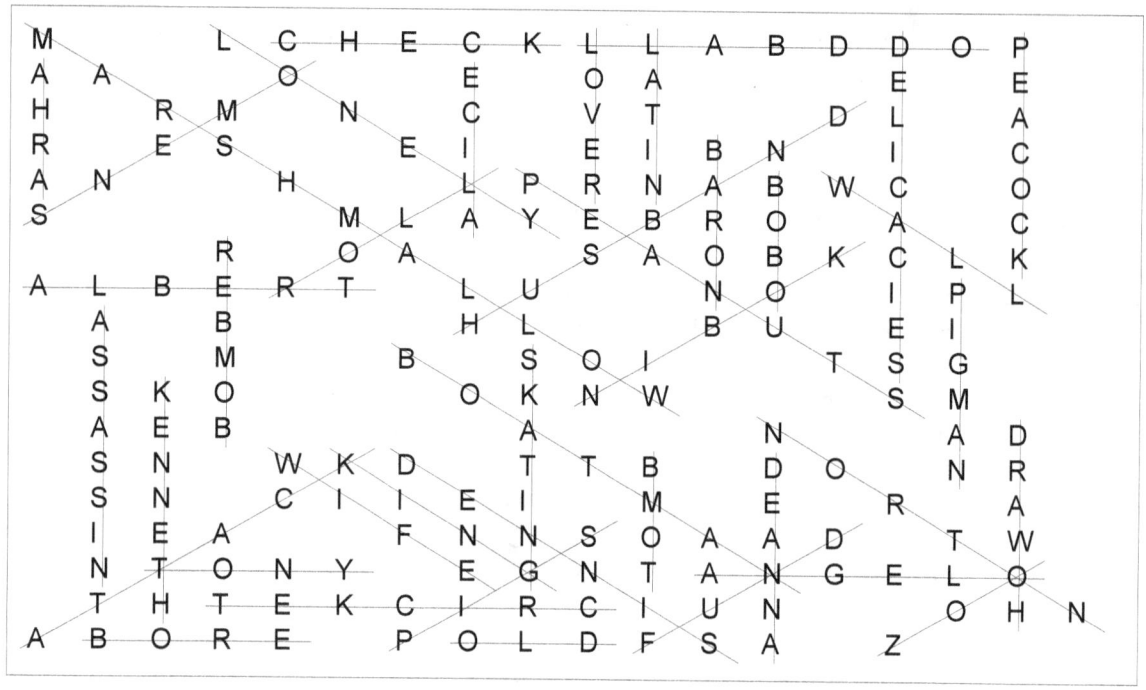

AHRA	DELICACIES	OLD
ALBERT	DENNIS	OMENS
ALICE	FUND	PEACOCK
ANGELO	HOWARD	PEANUTS
ASSASSIN	HUSBAND	PIGMAN
ATTACK	KENNETH	PIGS
BARON	KING	ROLL
BOATMAN	KOBIN	SKATING
BOBO	LATIN	TOMB
BOMBER	LONELY	TONY
BORE	LOVER	WALL
CHECK	MARSHMALLOW	WIFE
CRICKET	NORTON	ZOO
DEANNA	ODDBALL	

The Pigman Crossword 1

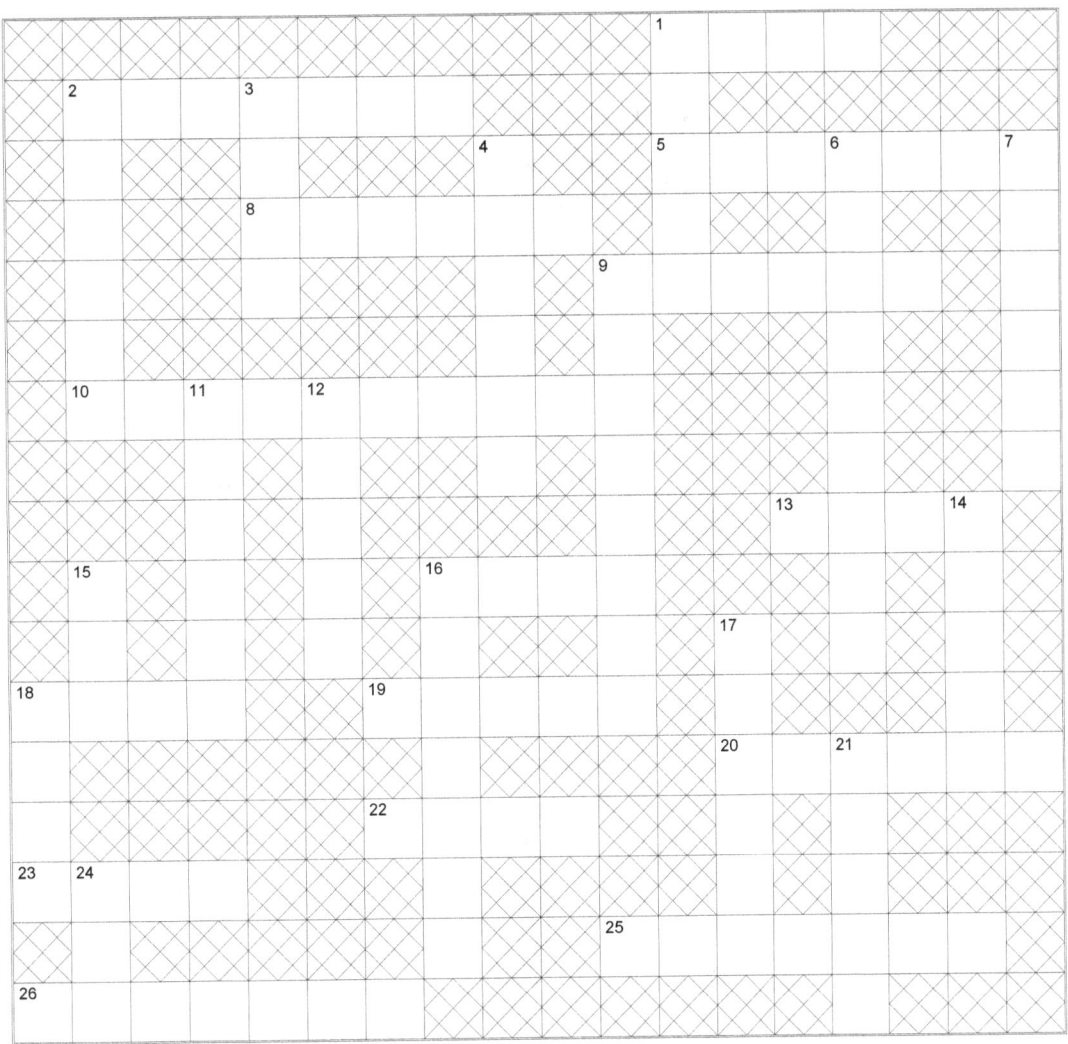

Across
1. 'Old maid' English teacher
2. Love
5. Magic
8. Bathroom ____
9. Mr. Pignati's first name
10. What Mr. Pignati buys J & L to eat
13. Supercolossal fruit ____
16. What Mr. Pignati collects
18. ___'s market; sells beer to anyone
19. Club Lorraine used as an excuse for not being home
20. The prince in a can
22. The L & J ___
23. The ___; John's father
25. Lorraine was attacked by a low IQ ___
26. ... get your hair cut. You look like an ___.

Down
1. Dennis's last name
2. Avenue; Mr. Pignati's street
3. A baboon
4. School friend of John & Lorraine
6. _____ marathon
7. Has a habit of shoplifting
9. Money
11. These people need visitors
12. Mr. Pignati gave the L&J fund one for $10
14. Sex
15. Bobo's home
16. Food for Bobo
17. She fixed the attendance cards for L & J
18. Masterson's ____
21. ____ Park Zoo
24. John's mother: ___ Lady

The Pigman Crossword 1 Answer Key

								1 K	I	N	G	
	2 H	U	3 S	B	A	N	D	O				
	O		O			4 D		5 B	O	6 A	T	M	A	7 N
	W		8 B	O	M	B	E	R	I		E		O
	A		O			N		9 A	N	G	E	L	O	R
	R					N		S			E		T
	10 D	11 E	12 L	I	C	A	C	I	E	S		P		O
			O		H			S		A		H		N
			N		E			S		S	13 R	O	14 L
	15 Z		E		C		16 P	I	G	S		N		O
	O		L		K		E			I	17 D	E		V
18 T	O	N	Y			19 L	A	T	I	N	E			E
O						N					20 A	L	21 B	E	R	T
M					22 F	U	N	D			N		A
23 B	24 O	R	E			T					N		R
	L					S		25 P	E	A	C	O	C	K
26 O	D	D	B	A	L	L							N

Across
1. 'Old maid' English teacher
2. Love
5. Magic
8. Bathroom ____
9. Mr. Pignati's first name
10. What Mr. Pignati buys J & L to eat
13. Supercolossal fruit ____
16. What Mr. Pignati collects
18. ___'s market; sells beer to anyone
19. Club Lorraine used as an excuse for not being home
20. The prince in a can
22. The L & J ___
23. The ___; John's father
25. Lorraine was attacked by a low IQ ___
26. ... get your hair cut. You look like an ___.

Down
1. Dennis's last name
2. Avenue; Mr. Pignati's street
3. A baboon
4. School friend of John & Lorraine
6. _____ marathon
7. Has a habit of shoplifting
9. Money
11. These people need visitors
12. Mr. Pignati gave the L&J fund one for $10
14. Sex
15. Bobo's home
16. Food for Bobo
17. She fixed the attendance cards for L & J
18. Masterson's ____
21. ____ Park Zoo
24. John's mother: ___ Lady

The Pigman Crossword 2

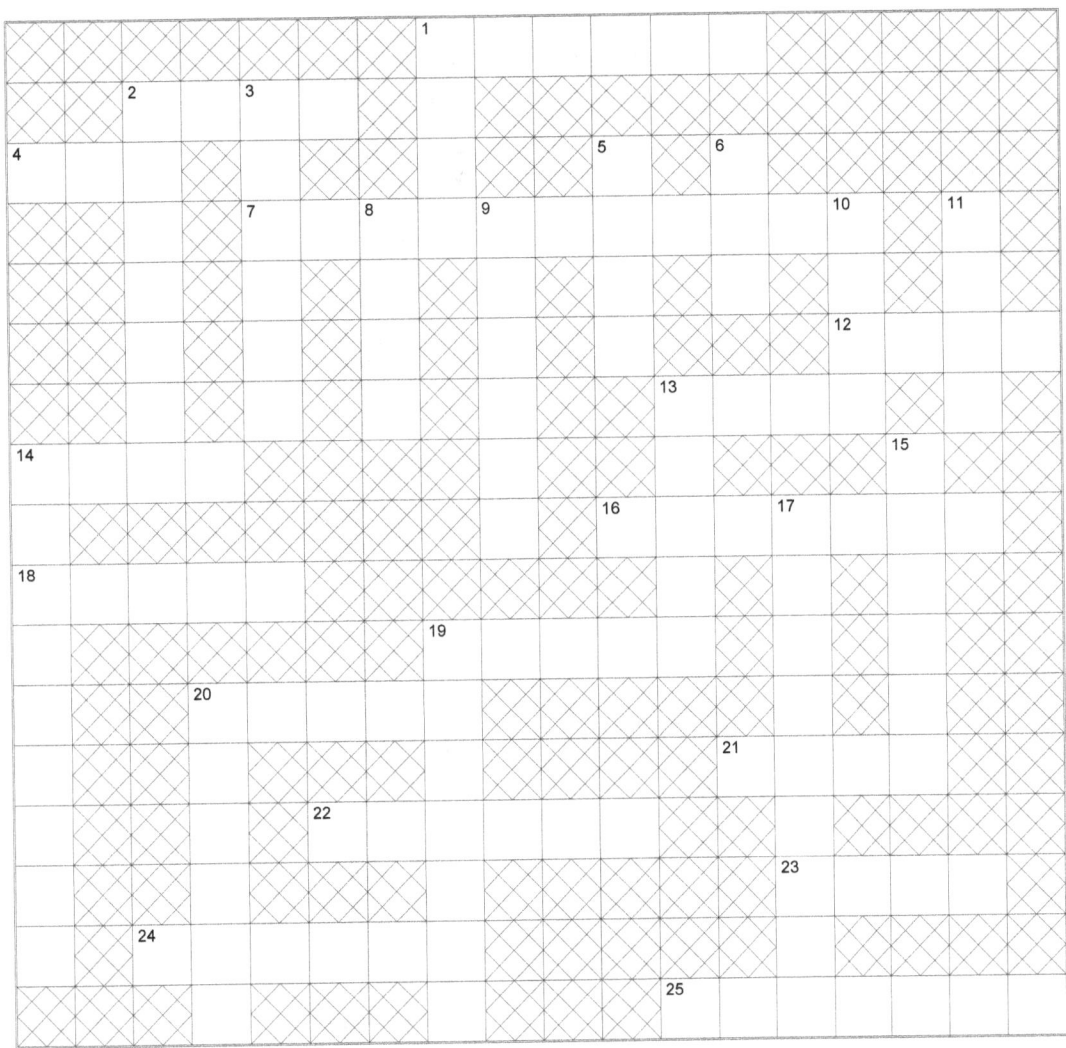

Across
1. Mr. Pignati
2. A baboon
4. Bobo's home
7. ____ Kid; Norton
12. The L & J ____
13. The ___; John's father
14. ___'s market; sells beer to anyone
16. The librarian
18. Sex
19. Dennis's last name
20. Dear ___
21. Aunt whose ghost gets blamed
22. School friend of John & Lorraine
23. Masterson's ____
24. The prince in a can
25. Food for Bobo

Down
1. What Mr. Pignati collects
2. Magic
3. Bathroom ____
5. Street where Kenneth works
6. John's mother: ___ Lady
8. Supercolossal fruit ____
9. Avenue; Mr. Pignati's street
10. Fun
11. 'Old maid' English teacher
13. ____ Park Zoo
14. _____ marathon
15. She fixed the attendance cards for L & J
17. Mrs. Pignati. She's not in California.
19. John's older brother
20. Mr. Pignati's first name

The Pigman Crossword 2 Answer Key

						¹P	I	G	M	A	N		
		²B	O	³B	O		I						
⁴Z	O	O		O			G		⁵W		⁶O		
		A		⁷M	A	⁸R	S	⁹H	M	A	L	L	O	W		¹⁰W		¹¹K
		T		B		O		O		L		D				I		I
		M		E		L		W		L				¹²F	U	N	D
		A		R		L		A		¹³B	O	R	E					G
¹⁴T	O	N	Y					R		A				¹⁵D		
E								D		¹⁶C	R	I	¹⁷C	K	E	T
¹⁸L	O	V	E	R						O			O			A
E						¹⁹K	O	B	I	N			N			N
P			²⁰A	L	I	C	E						C			N
H			N			N				²¹A	H	R	A	
O			G		²²D	E	N	N	I	S		E		
N			E			E						²³T	O	M	B
E		²⁴A	L	B	E	R	T					T		
			O			H				²⁵P	E	A	N	U	T	S

Across
1. Mr. Pignati
2. A baboon
4. Bobo's home
7. ____ Kid; Norton
12. The L & J ___
13. The ___; John's father
14. ___'s market; sells beer to anyone
16. The librarian
18. Sex
19. Dennis's last name
20. Dear ___
21. Aunt whose ghost gets blamed
22. School friend of John & Lorraine
23. Masterson's ____
24. The prince in a can
25. Food for Bobo

Down
1. What Mr. Pignati collects
2. Magic
3. Bathroom ____
5. Street where Kenneth works
6. John's mother: ___ Lady
8. Supercolossal fruit ____
9. Avenue; Mr. Pignati's street
10. Fun
11. 'Old maid' English teacher
13. ____ Park Zoo
14. _____ marathon
15. She fixed the attendance cards for L & J
17. Mrs. Pignati. She's not in California.
19. John's older brother
20. Mr. Pignati's first name

The Pigman Crossword 3

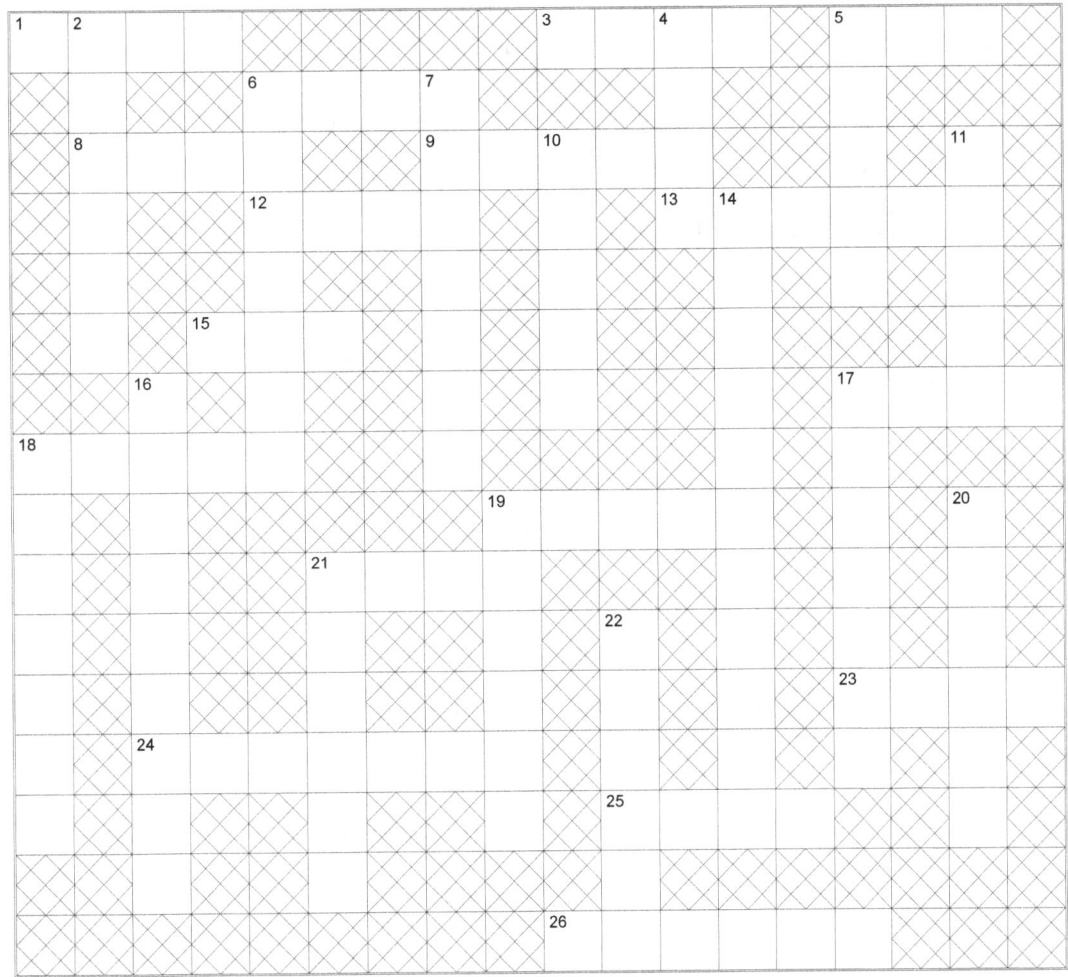

Across
1. Street where Kenneth works
3. Fun
5. John's mother: ___ Lady
6. What Mr. Pignati collects
8. The ___; John's father
9. Dennis's last name
12. Aunt whose ghost gets blamed
13. She fixed the attendance cards for L & J
15. Bobo's home
17. 'Old maid' English teacher
18. Mr. Pignati gave the L&J fund one for $10
19. Sex
21. A baboon
23. Masterson's ____
24. ... get your hair cut. You look like an ___.
25. ___'s market; sells beer to anyone
26. Mr. Pignati's first name

Down
2. The prince in a can
4. The L & J ___
5. Peanut lady, peacock, & nocturnal room were ___ of a bad day
6. Lorraine was attacked by a low IQ ___
7. Roller rink activity at Mr Pignati's house
10. ____ Park Zoo
11. Club Lorraine used as an excuse for not being home
14. Mr. Pignati's former occupation
16. _____ marathon
17. John's older brother
18. The librarian
19. These people need visitors
20. Mr. Pignati
21. Bathroom ____
22. Has a habit of shoplifting

The Pigman Crossword 3 Answer Key

	1 W	2 A	L	L				3 W	4 I	F	E		5 O	L	D
		L				6 P	7 S			U			M		
		8 B	O	R	E		9 K	O	10 B	I	N		E		11 L
		E			12 A	H	R	A		A		13 D	14 E	A	N	N	A
		R			C			T		R			L		S		T
		T		15 Z	O	O		I		O			E		S		I
			16 T		C			N		N			C		17 K	I	N	G
	18 C	H	E	C	K			G					T		E		
	R		L				19 L	O	V	E	R			N		20 P
	I		E		21 B	O	B	O				I		N		I
	C		P		O			N		22 N		C		E		G
	K		H		M			E		O		I		23 T	O	M	B
		24 O	D	D	B	A	L	L		R		A		H		A
	E		N		E			Y		25 T	O	N	Y			N
	T		E		R					O						
										26 A	N	G	E	L	O	

Across
1. Street where Kenneth works
3. Fun
5. John's mother: ___ Lady
6. What Mr. Pignati collects
8. The ___; John's father
9. Dennis's last name
12. Aunt whose ghost gets blamed
13. She fixed the attendance cards for L & J
15. Bobo's home
17. 'Old maid' English teacher
18. Mr. Pignati gave the L&J fund one for $10
19. Sex
21. A baboon
23. Masterson's ____
24. ... get your hair cut. You look like an ___.
25. ___'s market; sells beer to anyone
26. Mr. Pignati's first name

Down
2. The prince in a can
4. The L & J ___
5. Peanut lady, peacock, & nocturnal room were ___ of a bad day
6. Lorraine was attacked by a low IQ ___
7. Roller rink activity at Mr Pignati's house
10. ____ Park Zoo
11. Club Lorraine used as an excuse for not being home
14. Mr. Pignati's former occupation
16. _____ marathon
17. John's older brother
18. The librarian
19. These people need visitors
20. Mr. Pignati
21. Bathroom ____
22. Has a habit of shoplifting

The Pigman Crossword 4

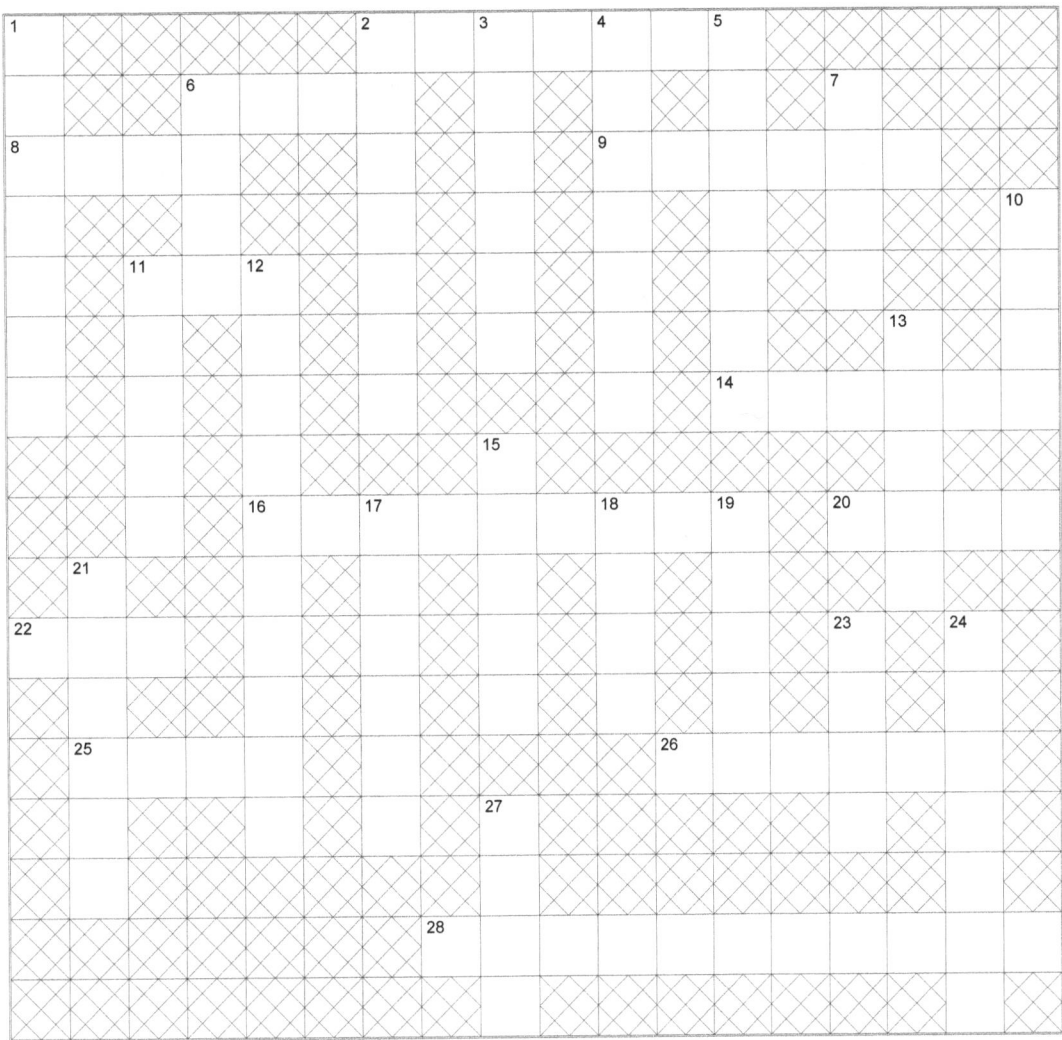

Across
2. Lorraine was attacked by a low IQ ___
6. Fun
8. Aunt whose ghost gets blamed
9. School friend of John & Lorraine
11. John's mother: ___ Lady
14. Avenue; Mr. Pignati's street
16. Mrs. Pignati. She's not in California.
20. A baboon
22. Bobo's home
25. The ___; John's father
26. She fixed the attendance cards for L & J
28. Mr. Pignati's former occupation

Down
1. Roller rink activity at Mr Pignati's house
2. Food for Bobo
3. Mr. Pignati had a heart ___
4. ... get your hair cut. You look like an ___.
5. John's older brother
6. Street where Kenneth works
7. What Mr. Pignati collects
10. The L & J ___
11. Peanut lady, peacock, & nocturnal room were ___ of a bad day
12. What Mr. Pignati buys J & L to eat
13. ___ Park Zoo
15. Mr. Pignati gave the L&J fund one for $10
17. Has a habit of shoplifting
18. ___'s market; sells beer to anyone
19. Dear ___
21. Bathroom ___
23. 'Old maid' English teacher
24. Magic
27. Supercolossal fruit ___

The Pigman Crossword 4 Answer Key

	1	2	3	4	5	6	7	8	9	10	11	12	13
1	S			2 P	3 E	A	C	O	C	K			
2	K		6 W	I	F	E		T		D		E		7 P
3	8 A	H	R	A		A		T		9 D	E	N	N	I	S
4	T			L		N		A		B		N		G		10 F
5	I		11 O	L	12 D		U		C		A		E		S		U
6	N		M		E		T		K		L		T		13 B		N
7	G		E		L		S		15 C		L		14 H	O	W	A	R	D
8			N		I				C						R		
9			S		16 C	17 O	N	C	H	18 E	T	19 T	A	20 B	O	B	O
10		21 B		A		O		E		T		O		L		N	
11	22 Z	O	O		C		R		C		N		I		23 K	24 B
12			M		I		T		K		Y		C		I		O
13			25 B	O	R	E		O				26 D	E	A	N	N	A
14			E		S		N		27 R						G		T
15			R						O								M
16								28 E	L	E	C	T	R	I	C	I	A	N
17									L								N

Across
2. Lorraine was attacked by a low IQ ___
6. Fun
8. Aunt whose ghost gets blamed
9. School friend of John & Lorraine
11. John's mother: ___ Lady
14. Avenue; Mr. Pignati's street
16. Mrs. Pignati. She's not in California.
20. A baboon
22. Bobo's home
25. The ___; John's father
26. She fixed the attendance cards for L & J
28. Mr. Pignati's former occupation

Down
1. Roller rink activity at Mr Pignati's house
2. Food for Bobo
3. Mr. Pignati had a heart ___
4. ... get your hair cut. You look like an ___.
5. John's older brother
6. Street where Kenneth works
7. What Mr. Pignati collects
10. The L & J ___
11. Peanut lady, peacock, & nocturnal room were ___ of a bad day
12. What Mr. Pignati buys J & L to eat
13. ____ Park Zoo
15. Mr. Pignati gave the L&J fund one for $10
17. Has a habit of shoplifting
18. ___'s market; sells beer to anyone
19. Dear ___
21. Bathroom ____
23. 'Old maid' English teacher
24. Magic
27. Supercolossal fruit ____

The Pigman

SKATING	BARON	PEACOCK	PEANUTS	ATTACK
ALBERT	CONCHETTA	ELECTRICIAN	MARSHMALLOW	PIGS
BOATMAN	AHRA	FREE SPACE	ALICE	KOBIN
KING	HOWARD	TELEPHONE	BORE	BOMBER
PIGMAN	ROLL	WALL	LONELY	DEANNA

The Pigman

DELICACIES	TONY	HUSBAND	LATIN	KENNETH
ZOO	ANGELO	FUND	NORTON	CRICKET
LOVER	DENNIS	FREE SPACE	BOBO	TOMB
WIFE	OLD	OMENS	ASSASSIN	DEANNA
LONELY	WALL	ROLL	PIGMAN	BOMBER

The Pigman

CONCHETTA	ODDBALL	KING	HOWARD	ATTACK
BOMBER	SKATING	FUND	KENNETH	LOVER
TOMB	HUSBAND	FREE SPACE	BOBO	BARON
DEANNA	WIFE	ELECTRICIAN	BORE	ZOO
OMENS	PEACOCK	CRICKET	MARSHMALLOW	DENNIS

The Pigman

AHRA	KOBIN	TELEPHONE	ASSASSIN	DELICACIES
CHECK	ALBERT	ROLL	ANGELO	PIGS
LATIN	LONELY	FREE SPACE	ALICE	PEANUTS
WALL	PIGMAN	TONY	BOATMAN	DENNIS
MARSHMALLOW	CRICKET	PEACOCK	OMENS	ZOO

The Pigman

HOWARD	KING	LOVER	ROLL	TONY
PIGMAN	OLD	KENNETH	ELECTRICIAN	CONCHETTA
PEACOCK	DEANNA	FREE SPACE	ATTACK	AHRA
PIGS	ANGELO	WALL	MARSHMALLOW	TELEPHONE
ZOO	LATIN	BOMBER	SKATING	ALICE

The Pigman

OMENS	ASSASSIN	NORTON	DENNIS	ALBERT
WIFE	BARON	LONELY	CRICKET	KOBIN
DELICACIES	BOBO	FREE SPACE	FUND	HUSBAND
BOATMAN	PEANUTS	CHECK	ODDBALL	ALICE
SKATING	BOMBER	LATIN	ZOO	TELEPHONE

The Pigman

ALICE	BOATMAN	TELEPHONE	ATTACK	KOBIN
MARSHMALLOW	LONELY	ANGELO	HUSBAND	AHRA
LOVER	TOMB	FREE SPACE	TONY	OLD
WIFE	HOWARD	FUND	KING	WALL
OMENS	PIGS	BARON	ODDBALL	BORE

The Pigman

BOBO	NORTON	CONCHETTA	DEANNA	SKATING
LATIN	CHECK	BOMBER	ELECTRICIAN	CRICKET
DENNIS	PEANUTS	FREE SPACE	ALBERT	PIGMAN
ASSASSIN	DELICACIES	PEACOCK	ROLL	BORE
ODDBALL	BARON	PIGS	OMENS	WALL

The Pigman

ALBERT	SKATING	ASSASSIN	AHRA	TONY
HUSBAND	TOMB	DELICACIES	KING	MARSHMALLOW
CRICKET	KENNETH	FREE SPACE	DEANNA	ZOO
FUND	PEACOCK	ROLL	ODDBALL	KOBIN
PIGMAN	LOVER	PIGS	OMENS	WALL

The Pigman

OLD	TELEPHONE	BOMBER	WIFE	ELECTRICIAN
BORE	LONELY	ATTACK	BARON	PEANUTS
CONCHETTA	BOATMAN	FREE SPACE	NORTON	BOBO
CHECK	DENNIS	LATIN	ANGELO	WALL
OMENS	PIGS	LOVER	PIGMAN	KOBIN

The Pigman

BORE	TONY	PIGMAN	BOATMAN	CHECK
DELICACIES	PIGS	DEANNA	AHRA	WIFE
MARSHMALLOW	ALICE	FREE SPACE	FUND	KOBIN
HOWARD	NORTON	ODDBALL	LOVER	ROLL
BOBO	LONELY	PEACOCK	ASSASSIN	DENNIS

The Pigman

ATTACK	LATIN	CRICKET	ANGELO	BARON
CONCHETTA	OLD	ALBERT	SKATING	HUSBAND
ELECTRICIAN	OMENS	FREE SPACE	BOMBER	KENNETH
PEANUTS	TELEPHONE	TOMB	WALL	DENNIS
ASSASSIN	PEACOCK	LONELY	BOBO	ROLL

The Pigman

MARSHMALLOW	BOMBER	ODDBALL	OLD	TOMB
WIFE	DENNIS	KOBIN	DEANNA	PIGS
KING	TELEPHONE	FREE SPACE	AHRA	LATIN
FUND	CRICKET	CHECK	PEACOCK	PEANUTS
ASSASSIN	ALBERT	ALICE	ANGELO	LONELY

The Pigman

KENNETH	BARON	SKATING	HOWARD	BOATMAN
ROLL	WALL	LOVER	DELICACIES	ZOO
ELECTRICIAN	OMENS	FREE SPACE	PIGMAN	TONY
NORTON	BORE	CONCHETTA	BOBO	LONELY
ANGELO	ALICE	ALBERT	ASSASSIN	PEANUTS

The Pigman

BOATMAN	DELICACIES	OLD	BARON	ASSASSIN
CONCHETTA	BOBO	WALL	DENNIS	ZOO
CRICKET	ELECTRICIAN	FREE SPACE	HUSBAND	ATTACK
ANGELO	AHRA	BOMBER	HOWARD	LONELY
ALBERT	KENNETH	PIGMAN	PEANUTS	ROLL

The Pigman

OMENS	MARSHMALLOW	ALICE	LOVER	FUND
NORTON	TOMB	KING	PIGS	TELEPHONE
ODDBALL	SKATING	FREE SPACE	KOBIN	LATIN
WIFE	PEACOCK	CHECK	TONY	ROLL
PEANUTS	PIGMAN	KENNETH	ALBERT	LONELY

The Pigman

LONELY	TONY	BARON	CRICKET	DENNIS
BOMBER	ANGELO	ATTACK	HOWARD	PEANUTS
ODDBALL	BORE	FREE SPACE	ROLL	ELECTRICIAN
CONCHETTA	PIGS	SKATING	OLD	ALICE
ZOO	FUND	DELICACIES	OMENS	AHRA

The Pigman

DEANNA	LOVER	WALL	KENNETH	HUSBAND
TELEPHONE	KING	MARSHMALLOW	WIFE	BOBO
ALBERT	BOATMAN	FREE SPACE	LATIN	NORTON
PEACOCK	TOMB	ASSASSIN	KOBIN	AHRA
OMENS	DELICACIES	FUND	ZOO	ALICE

The Pigman

ODDBALL	ATTACK	TONY	PEANUTS	KOBIN
DEANNA	ZOO	SKATING	KENNETH	BORE
FUND	AHRA	FREE SPACE	LATIN	KING
DENNIS	ROLL	WIFE	ALBERT	LOVER
OLD	CHECK	TELEPHONE	BARON	HOWARD

The Pigman

CRICKET	PEACOCK	MARSHMALLOW	ANGELO	CONCHETTA
HUSBAND	ASSASSIN	ELECTRICIAN	PIGS	OMENS
BOBO	BOATMAN	FREE SPACE	DELICACIES	TOMB
LONELY	WALL	BOMBER	PIGMAN	HOWARD
BARON	TELEPHONE	CHECK	OLD	LOVER

The Pigman

CRICKET	KING	ATTACK	FUND	ODDBALL
LONELY	BOATMAN	WALL	DELICACIES	AHRA
ROLL	CHECK	FREE SPACE	MARSHMALLOW	ALBERT
LATIN	CONCHETTA	OLD	HUSBAND	KENNETH
ANGELO	BOMBER	DEANNA	SKATING	PEANUTS

The Pigman

ASSASSIN	LOVER	ALICE	TOMB	BOBO
WIFE	DENNIS	PIGS	TELEPHONE	KOBIN
NORTON	ZOO	FREE SPACE	TONY	BARON
OMENS	PIGMAN	ELECTRICIAN	PEACOCK	PEANUTS
SKATING	DEANNA	BOMBER	ANGELO	KENNETH

The Pigman

ODDBALL	DELICACIES	CRICKET	BORE	LOVER
BOATMAN	KING	BOBO	FUND	CHECK
DENNIS	ATTACK	FREE SPACE	AHRA	CONCHETTA
ALBERT	TELEPHONE	PEANUTS	KENNETH	NORTON
DEANNA	HUSBAND	ZOO	OMENS	LONELY

The Pigman

ANGELO	OLD	ALICE	TONY	PIGMAN
ELECTRICIAN	KOBIN	HOWARD	PIGS	BARON
MARSHMALLOW	ROLL	FREE SPACE	ASSASSIN	TOMB
WIFE	PEACOCK	LATIN	SKATING	LONELY
OMENS	ZOO	HUSBAND	DEANNA	NORTON

The Pigman

TOMB	DEANNA	CONCHETTA	DELICACIES	KENNETH
KOBIN	DENNIS	BOBO	PIGS	ELECTRICIAN
BOATMAN	OLD	FREE SPACE	ZOO	ATTACK
ODDBALL	SKATING	BOMBER	NORTON	TONY
CHECK	HUSBAND	PEANUTS	BORE	FUND

The Pigman

PEACOCK	LOVER	ASSASSIN	CRICKET	TELEPHONE
BARON	LATIN	HOWARD	AHRA	OMENS
LONELY	PIGMAN	FREE SPACE	KING	WALL
ALBERT	MARSHMALLOW	ALICE	ANGELO	FUND
BORE	PEANUTS	HUSBAND	CHECK	TONY

The Pigman

PIGMAN	LOVER	TONY	CHECK	NORTON
BARON	OMENS	BOATMAN	KING	BOBO
DEANNA	MARSHMALLOW	FREE SPACE	WALL	ALBERT
ZOO	SKATING	ELECTRICIAN	AHRA	HOWARD
KOBIN	WIFE	CONCHETTA	KENNETH	TELEPHONE

The Pigman

FUND	PIGS	HUSBAND	BOMBER	LATIN
ASSASSIN	CRICKET	OLD	ANGELO	DELICACIES
PEANUTS	TOMB	FREE SPACE	ATTACK	ALICE
BORE	LONELY	ODDBALL	ROLL	TELEPHONE
KENNETH	CONCHETTA	WIFE	KOBIN	HOWARD

The Pigman

WALL	OLD	ODDBALL	BARON	SKATING
BOMBER	CRICKET	ELECTRICIAN	ZOO	PEACOCK
ASSASSIN	TONY	FREE SPACE	LATIN	KOBIN
KENNETH	HOWARD	ATTACK	DEANNA	WIFE
OMENS	BOATMAN	ANGELO	HUSBAND	NORTON

The Pigman

PIGMAN	MARSHMALLOW	LONELY	ALBERT	LOVER
PEANUTS	DELICACIES	ROLL	BORE	ALICE
CONCHETTA	KING	FREE SPACE	AHRA	DENNIS
PIGS	BOBO	CHECK	TOMB	NORTON
HUSBAND	ANGELO	BOATMAN	OMENS	WIFE

The Pigman

KING	DEANNA	PEANUTS	FUND	ELECTRICIAN
DENNIS	PIGS	TELEPHONE	HUSBAND	ALBERT
OLD	PEACOCK	FREE SPACE	KOBIN	ANGELO
ZOO	HOWARD	ROLL	KENNETH	TONY
AHRA	ASSASSIN	WIFE	BOMBER	ALICE

The Pigman

BOBO	OMENS	NORTON	LOVER	CHECK
BORE	WALL	LONELY	CRICKET	ATTACK
BARON	SKATING	FREE SPACE	CONCHETTA	DELICACIES
ODDBALL	PIGMAN	MARSHMALLOW	BOATMAN	ALICE
BOMBER	WIFE	ASSASSIN	AHRA	TONY

The Pigman Vocabulary Word List

No.	Word	Clue/Definition
1.	ADJUSTING	Fixing to a more compatible position
2.	AMOEBAE	A microscopic animal in water, soil & as a parasite in other animals
3.	ANALYZE	Examine methodically
4.	ANTAGONISTIC	Saying or doing things to intentionally annoy or displease someone
5.	ARTILLERY	Large caliber weapons
6.	AVOCATION	Hobby; work; profession
7.	BERSERK	Mentally or emotionally upset; deranged
8.	COMPENSATION	Offset; counterbalance; substitution
9.	CONGEALED	Stuck together; jelled; solidified
10.	DELIBERATELY	Intentionally; on purpose
11.	DISMEMBER	Divide into pieces
12.	EXAGGERATED	Enlarged or increased to an abnormal degree
13.	FIXATED	To become overly concerned with one subject
14.	GESTAPO	Police organization using terroristic methods
15.	GESTURED	Motioned with hands
16.	HEMOGLOBIN	Iron-containing respiratory pigment in red blood cells
17.	INCANDESCENT	Giving off visible light as a result of being heated
18.	INCONGRUOUS	Incompatible; not belonging together
19.	INGRATE	An ungrateful person
20.	INTIMATE	Close; personal
21.	MALADJUSTED	Not able to adjust to the demands of personal relationships
22.	MORTIFIED	Humiliated; embarrassed
23.	MULLED	Thought about; pondered
24.	MUNDANE	Ordinary; boring
25.	OSCILLOSCOPE	Electronic instrument that shows movements of voltage & currents
26.	PARANOIA	Extreme, irrational distrust of others
27.	PREDICAMENT	Troublesome situation
28.	PREVARICATIONS	Lies; statements straying from the truth
29.	PROFICIENCY	Competency; ability to do something well
30.	RELAPSES	Falling back to a former condition
31.	RITUAL	Ceremony; routine
32.	SCHIZOPHRENIC	Psychological disorder
33.	SUBSIDIZE	Give financial assistance to
34.	THROMBOSIS	Presence of a clot in a blood vessel
35.	TITMOUSE	Small insect-eating bird
36.	VOLUPTUOUS	Giving ample, unrestrained pleasure to the senses

The Pigman Vocabulary Fill In The Blanks 1

1. Divide into pieces
2. Large caliber weapons
3. Giving off visible light as a result of being heated
4. Give financial assistance to
5. Enlarged or increased to an abnormal degree
6. An ungrateful person
7. Electronic instrument that shows movements of voltage & currents
8. Motioned with hands
9. Humiliated; embarrassed
10. Competency; ability to do something well
11. Falling back to a former condition
12. Giving ample, unrestrained pleasure to the senses
13. Not able to adjust to the demands of personal relationships
14. Ceremony; routine
15. Intentionally; on purpose
16. Offset; counterbalance; substitution
17. Presence of a clot in a blood vessel
18. Extreme, irrational distrust of others
19. A microscopic animal in water, soil & as a parasite in other animals
20. Iron-containing respiratory pigment in red blood cells

The Pigman Vocabulary Fill In The Blanks 1 Answer Key

DISMEMBER	1. Divide into pieces
ARTILLERY	2. Large caliber weapons
INCANDESCENT	3. Giving off visible light as a result of being heated
SUBSIDIZE	4. Give financial assistance to
EXAGGERATED	5. Enlarged or increased to an abnormal degree
INGRATE	6. An ungrateful person
OSCILLOSCOPE	7. Electronic instrument that shows movements of voltage & currents
GESTURED	8. Motioned with hands
MORTIFIED	9. Humiliated; embarrassed
PROFICIENCY	10. Competency; ability to do something well
RELAPSES	11. Falling back to a former condition
VOLUPTUOUS	12. Giving ample, unrestrained pleasure to the senses
MALADJUSTED	13. Not able to adjust to the demands of personal relationships
RITUAL	14. Ceremony; routine
DELIBERATELY	15. Intentionally; on purpose
COMPENSATION	16. Offset; counterbalance; substitution
THROMBOSIS	17. Presence of a clot in a blood vessel
PARANOIA	18. Extreme, irrational distrust of others
AMOEBAE	19. A microscopic animal in water, soil & as a parasite in other animals
HEMOGLOBIN	20. Iron-containing respiratory pigment in red blood cells

The Pigman Vocabulary Fill In The Blanks 2

_____

_____

_____

_____

_____

_____

_____

_____

_____

_____

_____

_____

_____

_____

_____

_____

_____

_____

_____

_____

1. A microscopic animal in water, soil & as a parasite in other animals
2. Electronic instrument that shows movements of voltage & currents
3. Lies; statements straying from the truth
4. Presence of a clot in a blood vessel
5. Motioned with hands
6. Large caliber weapons
7. Iron-containing respiratory pigment in red blood cells
8. Mentally or emotionally upset; deranged
9. Enlarged or increased to an abnormal degree
10. Small insect-eating bird
11. Giving off visible light as a result of being heated
12. Psychological disorder
13. Fixing to a more compatible position
14. Examine methodically
15. Incompatible; not belonging together
16. Divide into pieces
17. An ungrateful person
18. Thought about; pondered
19. Not able to adjust to the demands of personal relationships
20. Extreme, irrational distrust of others

The Pigman Vocabulary Fill In The Blanks 2 Answer Key

AMOEBAE	1. A microscopic animal in water, soil & as a parasite in other animals
OSCILLOSCOPE	2. Electronic instrument that shows movements of voltage & currents
PREVARICATIONS	3. Lies; statements straying from the truth
THROMBOSIS	4. Presence of a clot in a blood vessel
GESTURED	5. Motioned with hands
ARTILLERY	6. Large caliber weapons
HEMOGLOBIN	7. Iron-containing respiratory pigment in red blood cells
BERSERK	8. Mentally or emotionally upset; deranged
EXAGGERATED	9. Enlarged or increased to an abnormal degree
TITMOUSE	10. Small insect-eating bird
INCANDESCENT	11. Giving off visible light as a result of being heated
SCHIZOPHRENIC	12. Psychological disorder
ADJUSTING	13. Fixing to a more compatible position
ANALYZE	14. Examine methodically
INCONGRUOUS	15. Incompatible; not belonging together
DISMEMBER	16. Divide into pieces
INGRATE	17. An ungrateful person
MULLED	18. Thought about; pondered
MALADJUSTED	19. Not able to adjust to the demands of personal relationships
PARANOIA	20. Extreme, irrational distrust of others

The Pigman Vocabulary Fill In The Blanks 3

1. Giving ample, unrestrained pleasure to the senses
2. Psychological disorder
3. Extreme, irrational distrust of others
4. Large caliber weapons
5. Incompatible; not belonging together
6. An ungrateful person
7. Presence of a clot in a blood vessel
8. Fixing to a more compatible position
9. Motioned with hands
10. Humiliated; embarrassed
11. A microscopic animal in water, soil & as a parasite in other animals
12. Lies; statements straying from the truth
13. Intentionally; on purpose
14. Falling back to a former condition
15. Electronic instrument that shows movements of voltage & currents
16. Ceremony; routine
17. Enlarged or increased to an abnormal degree
18. Competency; ability to do something well
19. Give financial assistance to
20. Offset; counterbalance; substitution

The Pigman Vocabulary Fill In The Blanks 3 Answer Key

VOLUPTUOUS	1. Giving ample, unrestrained pleasure to the senses
SCHIZOPHRENIC	2. Psychological disorder
PARANOIA	3. Extreme, irrational distrust of others
ARTILLERY	4. Large caliber weapons
INCONGRUOUS	5. Incompatible; not belonging together
INGRATE	6. An ungrateful person
THROMBOSIS	7. Presence of a clot in a blood vessel
ADJUSTING	8. Fixing to a more compatible position
GESTURED	9. Motioned with hands
MORTIFIED	10. Humiliated; embarrassed
AMOEBAE	11. A microscopic animal in water, soil & as a parasite in other animals
PREVARICATIONS	12. Lies; statements straying from the truth
DELIBERATELY	13. Intentionally; on purpose
RELAPSES	14. Falling back to a former condition
OSCILLOSCOPE	15. Electronic instrument that shows movements of voltage & currents
RITUAL	16. Ceremony; routine
EXAGGERATED	17. Enlarged or increased to an abnormal degree
PROFICIENCY	18. Competency; ability to do something well
SUBSIDIZE	19. Give financial assistance to
COMPENSATION	20. Offset; counterbalance; substitution

The Pigman Vocabulary Fill In The Blanks 4

_____

1. Offset; counterbalance; substitution

2. Ordinary; boring

3. Not able to adjust to the demands of personal relationships

4. Intentionally; on purpose

5. Give financial assistance to

6. A microscopic animal in water, soil & as a parasite in other animals

7. Giving off visible light as a result of being heated

8. An ungrateful person

9. Falling back to a former condition

10. Lies; statements straying from the truth

11. Thought about; pondered

12. Divide into pieces

13. Enlarged or increased to an abnormal degree

14. Small insect-eating bird

15. Humiliated; embarrassed

16. Ceremony; routine

17. To become overly concerned with one subject

18. Motioned with hands

19. Competency; ability to do something well

20. Large caliber weapons

The Pigman Vocabulary Fill In The Blanks 4 Answer Key

COMPENSATION	1. Offset; counterbalance; substitution
MUNDANE	2. Ordinary; boring
MALADJUSTED	3. Not able to adjust to the demands of personal relationships
DELIBERATELY	4. Intentionally; on purpose
SUBSIDIZE	5. Give financial assistance to
AMOEBAE	6. A microscopic animal in water, soil & as a parasite in other animals
INCANDESCENT	7. Giving off visible light as a result of being heated
INGRATE	8. An ungrateful person
RELAPSES	9. Falling back to a former condition
PREVARICATIONS	10. Lies; statements straying from the truth
MULLED	11. Thought about; pondered
DISMEMBER	12. Divide into pieces
EXAGGERATED	13. Enlarged or increased to an abnormal degree
TITMOUSE	14. Small insect-eating bird
MORTIFIED	15. Humiliated; embarrassed
RITUAL	16. Ceremony; routine
FIXATED	17. To become overly concerned with one subject
GESTURED	18. Motioned with hands
PROFICIENCY	19. Competency; ability to do something well
ARTILLERY	20. Large caliber weapons

The Pigman Vocabulary Matching 1

___ 1. GESTAPO
___ 2. OSCILLOSCOPE
___ 3. DELIBERATELY
___ 4. INCONGRUOUS
___ 5. RELAPSES
___ 6. ANALYZE
___ 7. THROMBOSIS
___ 8. INGRATE
___ 9. GESTURED
___ 10. ARTILLERY
___ 11. PREVARICATIONS
___ 12. MALADJUSTED
___ 13. PREDICAMENT
___ 14. ADJUSTING
___ 15. MULLED
___ 16. EXAGGERATED
___ 17. SCHIZOPHRENIC
___ 18. HEMOGLOBIN
___ 19. BERSERK
___ 20. TITMOUSE
___ 21. DISMEMBER
___ 22. INCANDESCENT
___ 23. FIXATED
___ 24. PARANOIA
___ 25. CONGEALED

A. Psychological disorder
B. An ungrateful person
C. Electronic instrument that shows movements of voltage & currents
D. Thought about; pondered
E. Stuck together; jelled; solidified
F. Mentally or emotionally upset; deranged
G. Enlarged or increased to an abnormal degree
H. Fixing to a more compatible position
I. Incompatible; not belonging together
J. Giving off visible light as a result of being heated
K. Falling back to a former condition
L. Motioned with hands
M. Not able to adjust to the demands of personal relationships
N. Examine methodically
O. Large caliber weapons
P. Police organization using terroristic methods
Q. Troublesome situation
R. Extreme, irrational distrust of others
S. Iron-containing respiratory pigment in red blood cells
T. Presence of a clot in a blood vessel
U. Lies; statements straying from the truth
V. To become overly concerned with one subject
W. Intentionally; on purpose
X. Divide into pieces
Y. Small insect-eating bird

The Pigman Vocabulary Matching 1 Answer Key

P - 1. GESTAPO	A. Psychological disorder
C - 2. OSCILLOSCOPE	B. An ungrateful person
W - 3. DELIBERATELY	C. Electronic instrument that shows movements of voltage & currents
I - 4. INCONGRUOUS	D. Thought about; pondered
K - 5. RELAPSES	E. Stuck together; jelled; solidified
N - 6. ANALYZE	F. Mentally or emotionally upset; deranged
T - 7. THROMBOSIS	G. Enlarged or increased to an abnormal degree
B - 8. INGRATE	H. Fixing to a more compatible position
L - 9. GESTURED	I. Incompatible; not belonging together
O - 10. ARTILLERY	J. Giving off visible light as a result of being heated
U - 11. PREVARICATIONS	K. Falling back to a former condition
M - 12. MALADJUSTED	L. Motioned with hands
Q - 13. PREDICAMENT	M. Not able to adjust to the demands of personal relationships
H - 14. ADJUSTING	N. Examine methodically
D - 15. MULLED	O. Large caliber weapons
G - 16. EXAGGERATED	P. Police organization using terroristic methods
A - 17. SCHIZOPHRENIC	Q. Troublesome situation
S - 18. HEMOGLOBIN	R. Extreme, irrational distrust of others
F - 19. BERSERK	S. Iron-containing respiratory pigment in red blood cells
Y - 20. TITMOUSE	T. Presence of a clot in a blood vessel
X - 21. DISMEMBER	U. Lies; statements straying from the truth
J - 22. INCANDESCENT	V. To become overly concerned with one subject
V - 23. FIXATED	W. Intentionally; on purpose
R - 24. PARANOIA	X. Divide into pieces
E - 25. CONGEALED	Y. Small insect-eating bird

The Pigman Vocabulary Matching 2

___ 1. AVOCATION   A. Hobby; work; profession
___ 2. FIXATED   B. Motioned with hands
___ 3. PREDICAMENT   C. Close; personal
___ 4. SCHIZOPHRENIC   D. Presence of a clot in a blood vessel
___ 5. ADJUSTING   E. Fixing to a more compatible position
___ 6. GESTURED   F. Giving ample, unrestrained pleasure to the senses
___ 7. INCANDESCENT   G. Incompatible; not belonging together
___ 8. VOLUPTUOUS   H. Ordinary; boring
___ 9. MALADJUSTED   I. Extreme, irrational distrust of others
___10. TITMOUSE   J. To become overly concerned with one subject
___11. ANTAGONISTIC   K. Mentally or emotionally upset; deranged
___12. MUNDANE   L. Large caliber weapons
___13. COMPENSATION   M. Not able to adjust to the demands of personal relationships
___14. PROFICIENCY   N. Lies; statements straying from the truth
___15. PREVARICATIONS   O. An ungrateful person
___16. ARTILLERY   P. Competency; ability to do something well
___17. AMOEBAE   Q. Psychological disorder
___18. INGRATE   R. Giving off visible light as a result of being heated
___19. PARANOIA   S. Saying or doing things to intentionally annoy or displease someone
___20. THROMBOSIS   T. A microscopic animal in water, soil & as a parasite in other animals
___21. INTIMATE   U. Offset; counterbalance; substitution
___22. INCONGRUOUS   V. Troublesome situation
___23. MORTIFIED   W. Humiliated; embarrassed
___24. SUBSIDIZE   X. Give financial assistance to
___25. BERSERK   Y. Small insect-eating bird

The Pigman Vocabulary Matching 2 Answer Key

A - 1.	AVOCATION	A. Hobby; work; profession
J - 2.	FIXATED	B. Motioned with hands
V - 3.	PREDICAMENT	C. Close; personal
Q - 4.	SCHIZOPHRENIC	D. Presence of a clot in a blood vessel
E - 5.	ADJUSTING	E. Fixing to a more compatible position
B - 6.	GESTURED	F. Giving ample, unrestrained pleasure to the senses
R - 7.	INCANDESCENT	G. Incompatible; not belonging together
F - 8.	VOLUPTUOUS	H. Ordinary; boring
M - 9.	MALADJUSTED	I. Extreme, irrational distrust of others
Y - 10.	TITMOUSE	J. To become overly concerned with one subject
S - 11.	ANTAGONISTIC	K. Mentally or emotionally upset; deranged
H - 12.	MUNDANE	L. Large caliber weapons
U - 13.	COMPENSATION	M. Not able to adjust to the demands of personal relationships
P - 14.	PROFICIENCY	N. Lies; statements straying from the truth
N - 15.	PREVARICATIONS	O. An ungrateful person
L - 16.	ARTILLERY	P. Competency; ability to do something well
T - 17.	AMOEBAE	Q. Psychological disorder
O - 18.	INGRATE	R. Giving off visible light as a result of being heated
I - 19.	PARANOIA	S. Saying or doing things to intentionally annoy or displease someone
D - 20.	THROMBOSIS	T. A microscopic animal in water, soil & as a parasite in other animals
C - 21.	INTIMATE	U. Offset; counterbalance; substitution
G - 22.	INCONGRUOUS	V. Troublesome situation
W - 23.	MORTIFIED	W. Humiliated; embarrassed
X - 24.	SUBSIDIZE	X. Give financial assistance to
K - 25.	BERSERK	Y. Small insect-eating bird

The Pigman Vocabulary Matching 3

___ 1. HEMOGLOBIN   A. Not able to adjust to the demands of personal relationships
___ 2. GESTAPO   B. Offset; counterbalance; substitution
___ 3. RELAPSES   C. Give financial assistance to
___ 4. MUNDANE   D. Intentionally; on purpose
___ 5. CONGEALED   E. Motioned with hands
___ 6. DELIBERATELY   F. Divide into pieces
___ 7. INCONGRUOUS   G. Falling back to a former condition
___ 8. VOLUPTUOUS   H. Ordinary; boring
___ 9. DISMEMBER   I. Thought about; pondered
___10. AMOEBAE   J. Lies; statements straying from the truth
___11. MALADJUSTED   K. Incompatible; not belonging together
___12. INGRATE   L. A microscopic animal in water, soil & as a parasite in other animals
___13. OSCILLOSCOPE   M. Police organization using terroristic methods
___14. PARANOIA   N. Iron-containing respiratory pigment in red blood cells
___15. MORTIFIED   O. Psychological disorder
___16. SCHIZOPHRENIC   P. Electronic instrument that shows movements of voltage & currents
___17. ARTILLERY   Q. Extreme, irrational distrust of others
___18. AVOCATION   R. An ungrateful person
___19. ADJUSTING   S. Giving ample, unrestrained pleasure to the senses
___20. MULLED   T. Hobby; work; profession
___21. SUBSIDIZE   U. Fixing to a more compatible position
___22. COMPENSATION   V. Stuck together; jelled; solidified
___23. THROMBOSIS   W. Large caliber weapons
___24. PREVARICATIONS   X. Presence of a clot in a blood vessel
___25. GESTURED   Y. Humiliated; embarrassed

The Pigman Vocabulary Matching 3 Answer Key

N - 1. HEMOGLOBIN
M - 2. GESTAPO
G - 3. RELAPSES
H - 4. MUNDANE
V - 5. CONGEALED
D - 6. DELIBERATELY
K - 7. INCONGRUOUS
S - 8. VOLUPTUOUS
F - 9. DISMEMBER
L - 10. AMOEBAE
A - 11. MALADJUSTED
R - 12. INGRATE
P - 13. OSCILLOSCOPE
Q - 14. PARANOIA
Y - 15. MORTIFIED
O - 16. SCHIZOPHRENIC
W - 17. ARTILLERY
T - 18. AVOCATION
U - 19. ADJUSTING
I - 20. MULLED
C - 21. SUBSIDIZE
B - 22. COMPENSATION
X - 23. THROMBOSIS
J - 24. PREVARICATIONS
E - 25. GESTURED

A. Not able to adjust to the demands of personal relationships
B. Offset; counterbalance; substitution
C. Give financial assistance to
D. Intentionally; on purpose
E. Motioned with hands
F. Divide into pieces
G. Falling back to a former condition
H. Ordinary; boring
I. Thought about; pondered
J. Lies; statements straying from the truth
K. Incompatible; not belonging together
L. A microscopic animal in water, soil & as a parasite in other animals
M. Police organization using terroristic methods
N. Iron-containing respiratory pigment in red blood cells
O. Psychological disorder
P. Electronic instrument that shows movements of voltage & currents
Q. Extreme, irrational distrust of others
R. An ungrateful person
S. Giving ample, unrestrained pleasure to the senses
T. Hobby; work; profession
U. Fixing to a more compatible position
V. Stuck together; jelled; solidified
W. Large caliber weapons
X. Presence of a clot in a blood vessel
Y. Humiliated; embarrassed

The Pigman Vocabulary Matching 4

___ 1. CONGEALED
___ 2. AVOCATION
___ 3. VOLUPTUOUS
___ 4. ANTAGONISTIC
___ 5. INGRATE
___ 6. GESTURED
___ 7. FIXATED
___ 8. OSCILLOSCOPE
___ 9. INCANDESCENT
___ 10. GESTAPO
___ 11. RELAPSES
___ 12. DISMEMBER
___ 13. ARTILLERY
___ 14. TITMOUSE
___ 15. INTIMATE
___ 16. PARANOIA
___ 17. DELIBERATELY
___ 18. THROMBOSIS
___ 19. AMOEBAE
___ 20. MALADJUSTED
___ 21. ANALYZE
___ 22. ADJUSTING
___ 23. EXAGGERATED
___ 24. PREDICAMENT
___ 25. PROFICIENCY

A. An ungrateful person
B. Electronic instrument that shows movements of voltage & currents
C. Falling back to a former condition
D. Close; personal
E. Divide into pieces
F. Extreme, irrational distrust of others
G. Large caliber weapons
H. Small insect-eating bird
I. Examine methodically
J. Giving off visible light as a result of being heated
K. Fixing to a more compatible position
L. Troublesome situation
M. Enlarged or increased to an abnormal degree
N. Stuck together; jelled; solidified
O. Hobby; work; profession
P. Presence of a clot in a blood vessel
Q. A microscopic animal in water, soil & as a parasite in other animals
R. Giving ample, unrestrained pleasure to the senses
S. Motioned with hands
T. Intentionally; on purpose
U. Not able to adjust to the demands of personal relationships
V. Competency; ability to do something well
W. To become overly concerned with one subject
X. Police organization using terroristic methods
Y. Saying or doing things to intentionally annoy or displease someone

The Pigman Vocabulary Matching 4 Answer Key

N - 1. CONGEALED		A. An ungrateful person
O - 2. AVOCATION		B. Electronic instrument that shows movements of voltage & currents
R - 3. VOLUPTUOUS		C. Falling back to a former condition
Y - 4. ANTAGONISTIC		D. Close; personal
A - 5. INGRATE		E. Divide into pieces
S - 6. GESTURED		F. Extreme, irrational distrust of others
W - 7. FIXATED		G. Large caliber weapons
B - 8. OSCILLOSCOPE		H. Small insect-eating bird
J - 9. INCANDESCENT		I. Examine methodically
X - 10. GESTAPO		J. Giving off visible light as a result of being heated
C - 11. RELAPSES		K. Fixing to a more compatible position
E - 12. DISMEMBER		L. Troublesome situation
G - 13. ARTILLERY		M. Enlarged or increased to an abnormal degree
H - 14. TITMOUSE		N. Stuck together; jelled; solidified
D - 15. INTIMATE		O. Hobby; work; profession
F - 16. PARANOIA		P. Presence of a clot in a blood vessel
T - 17. DELIBERATELY		Q. A microscopic animal in water, soil & as a parasite in other animals
P - 18. THROMBOSIS		R. Giving ample, unrestrained pleasure to the senses
Q - 19. AMOEBAE		S. Motioned with hands
U - 20. MALADJUSTED		T. Intentionally; on purpose
I - 21. ANALYZE		U. Not able to adjust to the demands of personal relationships
K - 22. ADJUSTING		V. Competency; ability to do something well
M - 23. EXAGGERATED		W. To become overly concerned with one subject
L - 24. PREDICAMENT		X. Police organization using terroristic methods
V - 25. PROFICIENCY		Y. Saying or doing things to intentionally annoy or displease someone

Copyrighted

The Pigman Vocabulary Magic Squares 1

Match the definition with the vocabulary word. Put your answers in the magic squares below. When your answers are correct, all columns and rows will add to the same number.

A. INGRATE
B. BERSERK
C. DELIBERATELY
D. PARANOIA
E. FIXATED
F. ARTILLERY
G. MORTIFIED
H. MUNDANE
I. PROFICIENCY
J. HEMOGLOBIN
K. SUBSIDIZE
L. COMPENSATION
M. VOLUPTUOUS
N. PREDICAMENT
O. INCANDESCENT
P. TITMOUSE

1. Ordinary; boring
2. Giving ample, unrestrained pleasure to the senses
3. Mentally or emotionally upset; deranged
4. Give financial assistance to
5. Iron-containing respiratory pigment in red blood cells
6. Intentionally; on purpose
7. Small insect-eating bird
8. To become overly concerned with one subject
9. Giving off visible light as a result of being heated
10. Large caliber weapons
11. Competency; ability to do something well
12. Extreme, irrational distrust of others
13. An ungrateful person
14. Offset; counterbalance; substitution
15. Humiliated; embarrassed
16. Troublesome situation

A=	B=	C=	D=
E=	F=	G=	H=
I=	J=	K=	L=
M=	N=	O=	P=

The Pigman Vocabulary Magic Squares 1 Answer Key

Match the definition with the vocabulary word. Put your answers in the magic squares below. When your answers are correct, all columns and rows will add to the same number.

A. INGRATE
B. BERSERK
C. DELIBERATELY
D. PARANOIA
E. FIXATED
F. ARTILLERY
G. MORTIFIED
H. MUNDANE
I. PROFICIENCY
J. HEMOGLOBIN
K. SUBSIDIZE
L. COMPENSATION
M. VOLUPTUOUS
N. PREDICAMENT
O. INCANDESCENT
P. TITMOUSE

1. Ordinary; boring
2. Giving ample, unrestrained pleasure to the senses
3. Mentally or emotionally upset; deranged
4. Give financial assistance to
5. Iron-containing respiratory pigment in red blood cells
6. Intentionally; on purpose
7. Small insect-eating bird
8. To become overly concerned with one subject
9. Giving off visible light as a result of being heated
10. Large caliber weapons
11. Competency; ability to do something well
12. Extreme, irrational distrust of others
13. An ungrateful person
14. Offset; counterbalance; substitution
15. Humiliated; embarrassed
16. Troublesome situation

A=13	B=3	C=6	D=12
E=8	F=10	G=15	H=1
I=11	J=5	K=4	L=14
M=2	N=16	O=9	P=7

The Pigman Vocabulary Magic Squares 2

Match the definition with the vocabulary word. Put your answers in the magic squares below. When your answers are correct, all columns and rows will add to the same number.

A. RELAPSES
B. TITMOUSE
C. CONGEALED
D. GESTAPO
E. PREVARICATIONS
F. GESTURED
G. FIXATED
H. RITUAL
I. INCANDESCENT
J. SUBSIDIZE
K. SCHIZOPHRENIC
L. ANTAGONISTIC
M. AVOCATION
N. ANALYZE
O. MORTIFIED
P. PREDICAMENT

1. Ceremony; routine
2. Falling back to a former condition
3. Small insect-eating bird
4. To become overly concerned with one subject
5. Give financial assistance to
6. Humiliated; embarrassed
7. Troublesome situation
8. Giving off visible light as a result of being heated
9. Psychological disorder
10. Examine methodically
11. Hobby; work; profession
12. Saying or doing things to intentionally annoy or displease someone
13. Lies; statements straying from the truth
14. Police organization using terroristic methods
15. Stuck together; jelled; solidified
16. Motioned with hands

A=	B=	C=	D=
E=	F=	G=	H=
I=	J=	K=	L=
M=	N=	O=	P=

The Pigman Vocabulary Magic Squares 2 Answer Key

Match the definition with the vocabulary word. Put your answers in the magic squares below. When your answers are correct, all columns and rows will add to the same number.

A. RELAPSES
B. TITMOUSE
C. CONGEALED
D. GESTAPO
E. PREVARICATIONS
F. GESTURED
G. FIXATED
H. RITUAL
I. INCANDESCENT
J. SUBSIDIZE
K. SCHIZOPHRENIC
L. ANTAGONISTIC
M. AVOCATION
N. ANALYZE
O. MORTIFIED
P. PREDICAMENT

1. Ceremony; routine
2. Falling back to a former condition
3. Small insect-eating bird
4. To become overly concerned with one subject
5. Give financial assistance to
6. Humiliated; embarrassed
7. Troublesome situation
8. Giving off visible light as a result of being heated
9. Psychological disorder
10. Examine methodically
11. Hobby; work; profession
12. Saying or doing things to intentionally annoy or displease someone
13. Lies; statements straying from the truth
14. Police organization using terroristic methods
15. Stuck together; jelled; solidified
16. Motioned with hands

A=2	B=3	C=15	D=14
E=13	F=16	G=4	H=1
I=8	J=5	K=9	L=12
M=11	N=10	O=6	P=7

The Pigman Vocabulary Magic Squares 3

Match the definition with the vocabulary word. Put your answers in the magic squares below. When your answers are correct, all columns and rows will add to the same number.

A. CONGEALED
B. ADJUSTING
C. GESTAPO
D. INCONGRUOUS
E. THROMBOSIS
F. VOLUPTUOUS
G. EXAGGERATED
H. AVOCATION
I. BERSERK
J. HEMOGLOBIN
K. INCANDESCENT
L. DISMEMBER
M. PREVARICATIONS
N. MULLED
O. MUNDANE
P. SCHIZOPHRENIC

1. Stuck together; jelled; solidified
2. Thought about; pondered
3. Iron-containing respiratory pigment in red blood cells
4. Presence of a clot in a blood vessel
5. Enlarged or increased to an abnormal degree
6. Divide into pieces
7. Psychological disorder
8. Police organization using terroristic methods
9. Ordinary; boring
10. Incompatible; not belonging together
11. Hobby; work; profession
12. Giving off visible light as a result of being heated
13. Mentally or emotionally upset; deranged
14. Giving ample, unrestrained pleasure to the senses
15. Fixing to a more compatible position
16. Lies; statements straying from the truth

A=	B=	C=	D=
E=	F=	G=	H=
I=	J=	K=	L=
M=	N=	O=	P=

The Pigman Vocabulary Magic Squares 3 Answer Key

Match the definition with the vocabulary word. Put your answers in the magic squares below. When your answers are correct, all columns and rows will add to the same number.

A. CONGEALED
B. ADJUSTING
C. GESTAPO
D. INCONGRUOUS
E. THROMBOSIS
F. VOLUPTUOUS
G. EXAGGERATED
H. AVOCATION
I. BERSERK
J. HEMOGLOBIN
K. INCANDESCENT
L. DISMEMBER
M. PREVARICATIONS
N. MULLED
O. MUNDANE
P. SCHIZOPHRENIC

1. Stuck together; jelled; solidified
2. Thought about; pondered
3. Iron-containing respiratory pigment in red blood cells
4. Presence of a clot in a blood vessel
5. Enlarged or increased to an abnormal degree
6. Divide into pieces
7. Psychological disorder
8. Police organization using terroristic methods
9. Ordinary; boring
10. Incompatible; not belonging together
11. Hobby; work; profession
12. Giving off visible light as a result of being heated
13. Mentally or emotionally upset; deranged
14. Giving ample, unrestrained pleasure to the senses
15. Fixing to a more compatible position
16. Lies; statements straying from the truth

A=1	B=15	C=8	D=10
E=4	F=14	G=5	H=11
I=13	J=3	K=12	L=6
M=16	N=2	O=9	P=7

The Pigman Vocabulary Magic Squares 4

Match the definition with the vocabulary word. Put your answers in the magic squares below. When your answers are correct, all columns and rows will add to the same number.

A. TITMOUSE
B. INTIMATE
C. INCONGRUOUS
D. DELIBERATELY
E. MUNDANE
F. INCANDESCENT
G. SCHIZOPHRENIC
H. BERSERK
I. SUBSIDIZE
J. INGRATE
K. AVOCATION
L. EXAGGERATED
M. HEMOGLOBIN
N. MORTIFIED
O. FIXATED
P. OSCILLOSCOPE

1. To become overly concerned with one subject
2. Intentionally; on purpose
3. An ungrateful person
4. Ordinary; boring
5. Give financial assistance to
6. Giving off visible light as a result of being heated
7. Electronic instrument that shows movements of voltage & currents
8. Incompatible; not belonging together
9. Mentally or emotionally upset; deranged
10. Hobby; work; profession
11. Small insect-eating bird
12. Humiliated; embarrassed
13. Close; personal
14. Iron-containing respiratory pigment in red blood cells
15. Psychological disorder
16. Enlarged or increased to an abnormal degree

A=	B=	C=	D=
E=	F=	G=	H=
I=	J=	K=	L=
M=	N=	O=	P=

The Pigman Vocabulary Magic Squares 4 Answer Key

Match the definition with the vocabulary word. Put your answers in the magic squares below. When your answers are correct, all columns and rows will add to the same number.

A. TITMOUSE
B. INTIMATE
C. INCONGRUOUS
D. DELIBERATELY
E. MUNDANE
F. INCANDESCENT
G. SCHIZOPHRENIC
H. BERSERK
I. SUBSIDIZE
J. INGRATE
K. AVOCATION
L. EXAGGERATED
M. HEMOGLOBIN
N. MORTIFIED
O. FIXATED
P. OSCILLOSCOPE

1. To become overly concerned with one subject
2. Intentionally; on purpose
3. An ungrateful person
4. Ordinary; boring
5. Give financial assistance to
6. Giving off visible light as a result of being heated
7. Electronic instrument that shows movements of voltage & currents
8. Incompatible; not belonging together
9. Mentally or emotionally upset; deranged
10. Hobby; work; profession
11. Small insect-eating bird
12. Humiliated; embarrassed
13. Close; personal
14. Iron-containing respiratory pigment in red blood cells
15. Psychological disorder
16. Enlarged or increased to an abnormal degree

A=11	B=13	C=8	D=2
E=4	F=6	G=15	H=9
I=5	J=3	K=10	L=16
M=14	N=12	O=1	P=7

The Pigman Vocabulary Word Search 1

Words are placed backwards, forward, diagonally, up and down. Clues listed below can help you find the words. Circle the hidden vocabulary words in the maze.

F	I	N	T	I	M	A	T	E	T	H	R	O	M	B	O	S	I	S	S
I	R	I	T	U	A	L	D	H	P	R	E	D	I	C	A	M	E	N	T
X	D	H	F	D	B	E	Z	H	C	R	C	M	Y	V	M	E	Y	R	V
A	C	N	D	D	R	A	W	F	C	O	N	C	O	F	G	A	H	B	S
T	O	Y	E	U	A	R	Q	N	R	R	N	B	N	G	K	B	V	B	K
E	M	W	T	D	V	T	P	F	S	Y	G	G	Z	R	L	E	S	C	W
D	P	S	A	I	O	I	N	G	R	A	T	E	E	K	Z	O	H	F	Y
Y	E	U	R	S	C	L	J	J	M	G	Z	S	S	A	X	M	B	J	D
G	N	O	E	M	A	L	Y	K	Z	Y	R	U	P	T	L	A	S	I	F
N	S	U	G	E	T	E	X	Z	L	E	E	O	R	M	A	E	X	M	N
I	A	R	G	M	I	R	M	A	B	E	L	M	O	O	M	P	D	A	J
T	T	G	A	B	O	Y	N	C	N	Z	A	T	F	R	U	A	O	L	S
S	I	N	X	E	N	A	F	A	L	I	P	I	I	T	L	R	B	A	V
U	O	O	E	R	D	P	D	F	B	D	S	T	C	I	L	A	B	D	L
J	N	C	K	L	P	N	D	J	P	I	E	X	I	F	E	N	L	J	J
D	M	N	F	F	U	G	K	B	W	S	S	F	E	I	D	O	T	U	D
A	Q	I	G	M	V	R	V	B	N	B	P	Q	N	E	F	I	D	S	C
V	O	L	U	P	T	U	O	U	S	U	M	Y	C	D	L	A	B	T	J
E	P	O	C	S	O	L	L	I	C	S	O	B	Y	V	D	Z	R	E	D
S	C	H	I	Z	O	P	H	R	E	N	I	C	R	Q	B	F	G	D	D

A microscopic animal in water, soil & as a parasite in other animals (7)
An ungrateful person (7)
Ceremony; routine (6)
Psychological disorder(13)

Close; personal (8)
Competency; ability to do something well (11)
Divide into pieces (9)
Electronic instrument that shows movements of voltage & currents (12)
Enlarged or increased to an abnormal degree (11)
Examine methodically (7)
Extreme, irrational distrust of others (8)
Falling back to a former condition (8)
Fixing to a more compatible position (9)
Give financial assistance to (9)
Giving ample, unrestrained pleasure to the senses (10)

Hobby; work; profession (9)
Humiliated; embarrassed (9)
Incompatible; not belonging together (11)
Iron-containing respiratory pigment in red blood cells (10)
Large caliber weapons (9)
Mentally or emotionally upset; deranged (7)
Motioned with hands (8)
Not able to adjust to the demands of personal relationships (11)
Offset; counterbalance; substitution (12)
Ordinary; boring (7)
Police organization using terroristic methods (7)
Presence of a clot in a blood vessel (10)
Small insect-eating bird (8)
Stuck together; jelled; solidified (9)
Thought about; pondered (6)
To become overly concerned with one subject (7)
Troublesome situation (11)

The Pigman Vocabulary Word Search 1 Answer Key

Words are placed backwards, forward, diagonally, up and down. Clues listed below can help you find the words. Circle the hidden vocabulary words in the maze.

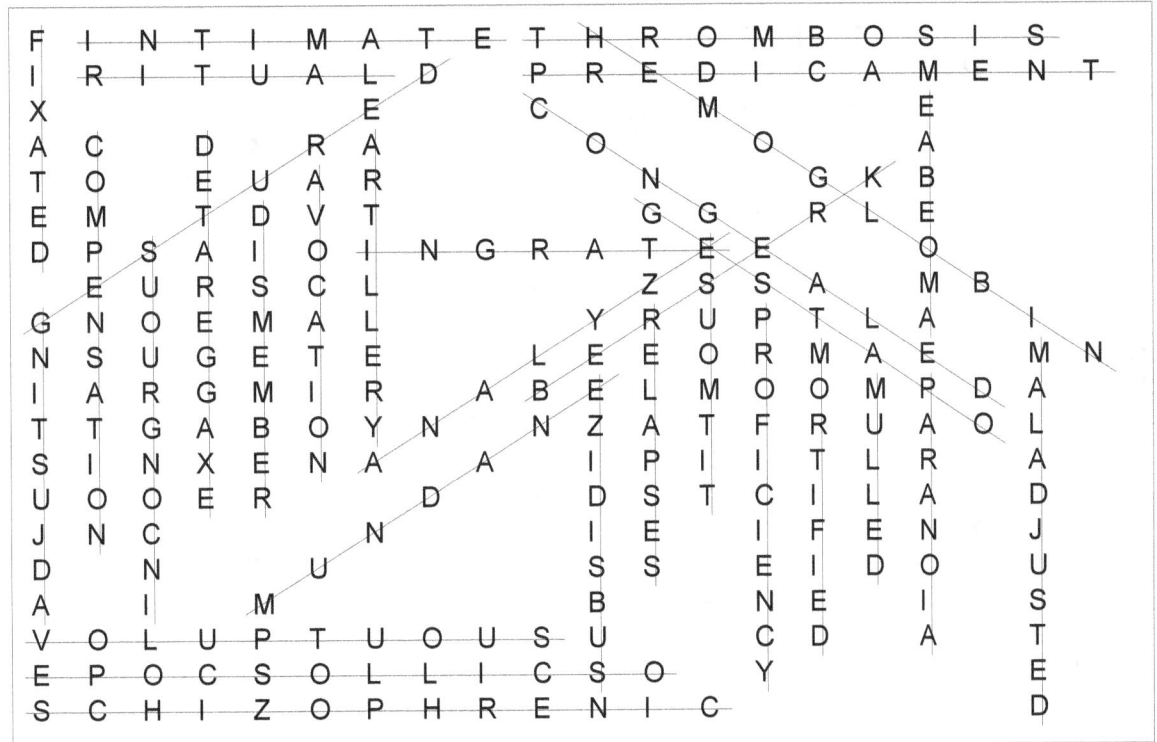

A microscopic animal in water, soil & as a parasite in other animals (7)
An ungrateful person (7)
Ceremony; routine (6)
Psychological disorder (13)

Close; personal (8)
Competency; ability to do something well (11)
Divide into pieces (9)
Electronic instrument that shows movements of voltage & currents (12)
Enlarged or increased to an abnormal degree (11)
Examine methodically (7)
Extreme, irrational distrust of others (8)
Falling back to a former condition (8)
Fixing to a more compatible position (9)
Give financial assistance to (9)
Giving ample, unrestrained pleasure to the senses (10)

Hobby; work; profession (9)
Humiliated; embarrassed (9)
Incompatible; not belonging together (11)
Iron-containing respiratory pigment in red blood cells (10)
Large caliber weapons (9)
Mentally or emotionally upset; deranged (7)
Motioned with hands (8)
Not able to adjust to the demands of personal relationships (11)
Offset; counterbalance; substitution (12)
Ordinary; boring (7)
Police organization using terroristic methods (7)
Presence of a clot in a blood vessel (10)
Small insect-eating bird (8)
Stuck together; jelled; solidified (9)
Thought about; pondered (6)
To become overly concerned with one subject (7)
Troublesome situation (11)

The Pigman Vocabulary Word Search 2

Words are placed backwards, forward, diagonally, up and down. Clues listed below can help you find the words. Circle the hidden vocabulary words in the maze.

```
S U O U R G N O C N I D E I F I T R O M
Y M K P P R O F I C I E N C Y R I S X T
S Y K A G Q M B Y Q W J M G D F T P D N
C L B R R C O N G E A L E D Y S M Z Y L
H E D A D L R C E J F I S L H I O M M J
I T W N G Y X N S T S S N H P S U V G F
Z A L O T W Q M T T E J N T E O S Z E F
O R M I W Y Z D A S R H O Z I B E H S Z
P E T A R G N I P R E D I C A M E N T X
H B X T D B F A O A P D T N R O A C U J
R I Q A F J L H B N I C A O T R V T R B
E L J K G E U E F S J L S I I H O R E G
N E M F R G O S B C Y T N L T L I D P
I D Z V W M E U T Z R Q E A L F U T X X
C S P K A D S R E I X C P C E I P U Y Y
B E R S E R K T A Z N V M O R X T A W F
T R H L N F B M C T J G O V Y A U L S J
P J L D I S M E M B E R C A R T O V S W
M U N D A N E H Q J C D R M B E U W F M
M A L A D J U S T E D Z Q F Y D S R W F
```

A microscopic animal in water, soil & as a parasite in other animals (7)
An ungrateful person (7)
Ceremony; routine (6)
Psychological disorder (13)

Close; personal (8)
Competency; ability to do something well (11)
Divide into pieces (9)
Enlarged or increased to an abnormal degree (11)
Examine methodically (7)
Extreme, irrational distrust of others (8)
Falling back to a former condition (8)
Fixing to a more compatible position (9)
Give financial assistance to (9)
Giving ample, unrestrained pleasure to the senses (10)
Hobby; work; profession (9)
Humiliated; embarrassed (9)

Incompatible; not belonging together (11)
Intentionally; on purpose (12)
Iron-containing respiratory pigment in red blood cells (10)
Large caliber weapons (9)
Mentally or emotionally upset; deranged (7)
Motioned with hands (8)
Not able to adjust to the demands of personal relationships (11)
Offset; counterbalance; substitution (12)
Ordinary; boring (7)
Police organization using terroristic methods (7)
Presence of a clot in a blood vessel (10)
Small insect-eating bird (8)
Stuck together; jelled; solidified (9)
Thought about; pondered (6)
To become overly concerned with one subject (7)
Troublesome situation (11)

The Pigman Vocabulary Word Search 2 Answer Key

Words are placed backwards, forward, diagonally, up and down. Clues listed below can help you find the words. Circle the hidden vocabulary words in the maze.

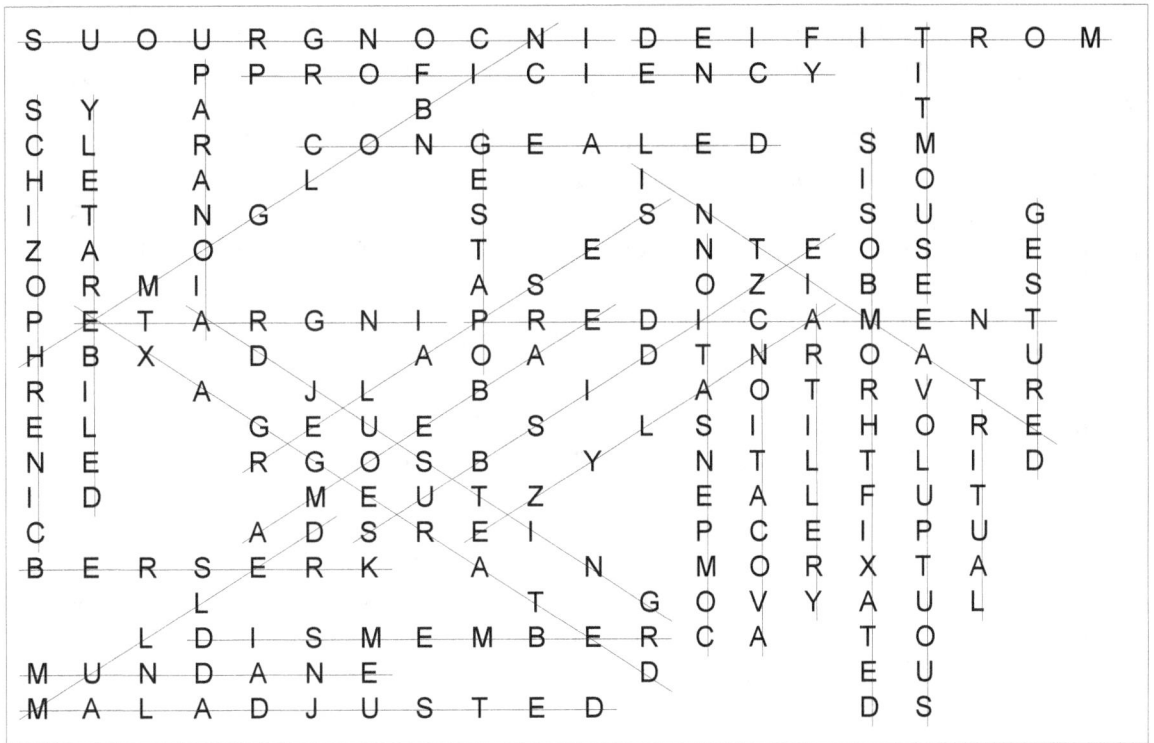

A microscopic animal in water, soil & as a parasite in other animals (7)
An ungrateful person (7)
Ceremony; routine (6)
Psychological disorder (13)

Close; personal (8)
Competency; ability to do something well (11)
Divide into pieces (9)
Enlarged or increased to an abnormal degree (11)
Examine methodically (7)
Extreme, irrational distrust of others (8)
Falling back to a former condition (8)
Fixing to a more compatible position (9)
Give financial assistance to (9)
Giving ample, unrestrained pleasure to the senses (10)
Hobby; work; profession (9)
Humiliated; embarrassed (9)

Incompatible; not belonging together (11)
Intentionally; on purpose (12)
Iron-containing respiratory pigment in red blood cells (10)
Large caliber weapons (9)
Mentally or emotionally upset; deranged (7)
Motioned with hands (8)
Not able to adjust to the demands of personal relationships (11)
Offset; counterbalance; substitution (12)
Ordinary; boring (7)
Police organization using terroristic methods (7)
Presence of a clot in a blood vessel (10)
Small insect-eating bird (8)
Stuck together; jelled; solidified (9)
Thought about; pondered (6)
To become overly concerned with one subject (7)
Troublesome situation (11)

The Pigman Vocabulary Word Search 3

Words are placed backwards, forward, diagonally, up and down. Words listed below are included in the maze. Circle the hidden vocabulary words in the maze.

```
T I T M O U S E Z Y L A N A G O D V R C
G Q S H R V D L Q R V R Q M S I E O E X
G Z U B R S T D V O Q T C C B N T L L T
Y E B M G O X N C G T I I M E T S U A J
Q N S Q Y S M A C C M L T U R I U P P L
B J I T C G T B D Q L L S L S M J T S G
Y R D Y U I Q G O O T E I L E A D U E P
K R I V O R B V S S Y R N E R T A O S X
H N Z N G R E C W S I Y O D K E L U Z Y
E E E L N H O D G U T S G H S D A S J D
X L M R V P T X V O E N A D N U M N I J
A M V O E F A F H U C Z T M V D J S F H
G O G T G K F R M R R X N N E N M A I W
G R L D Q L N P A G S J A L V E M R X Z
E T G Y P P O P T N W F A X M O R I A Z
R I Q N T B G B Z O O E Q B E N P T T B
A F M G X W V S I C G I E B F Y N U E N
T I A D J U S T I N G R A T E P F A D C
E E V W K H Z S O I V E M W M V H L T B
D D P R O F I C I E N C Y G E S T A P O
```

ADJUSTING	FIXATED	MUNDANE
AMOEBAE	GESTAPO	OSCILLOSCOPE
ANALYZE	GESTURED	PARANOIA
ANTAGONISTIC	HEMOGLOBIN	PROFICIENCY
ARTILLERY	INCONGRUOUS	RELAPSES
AVOCATION	INGRATE	RITUAL
BERSERK	INTIMATE	SUBSIDIZE
CONGEALED	MALADJUSTED	THROMBOSIS
DISMEMBER	MORTIFIED	TITMOUSE
EXAGGERATED	MULLED	VOLUPTUOUS

The Pigman Vocabulary Word Search 3 Answer Key

Words are placed backwards, forward, diagonally, up and down. Words listed below are included in the maze. Circle the hidden vocabulary words in the maze.

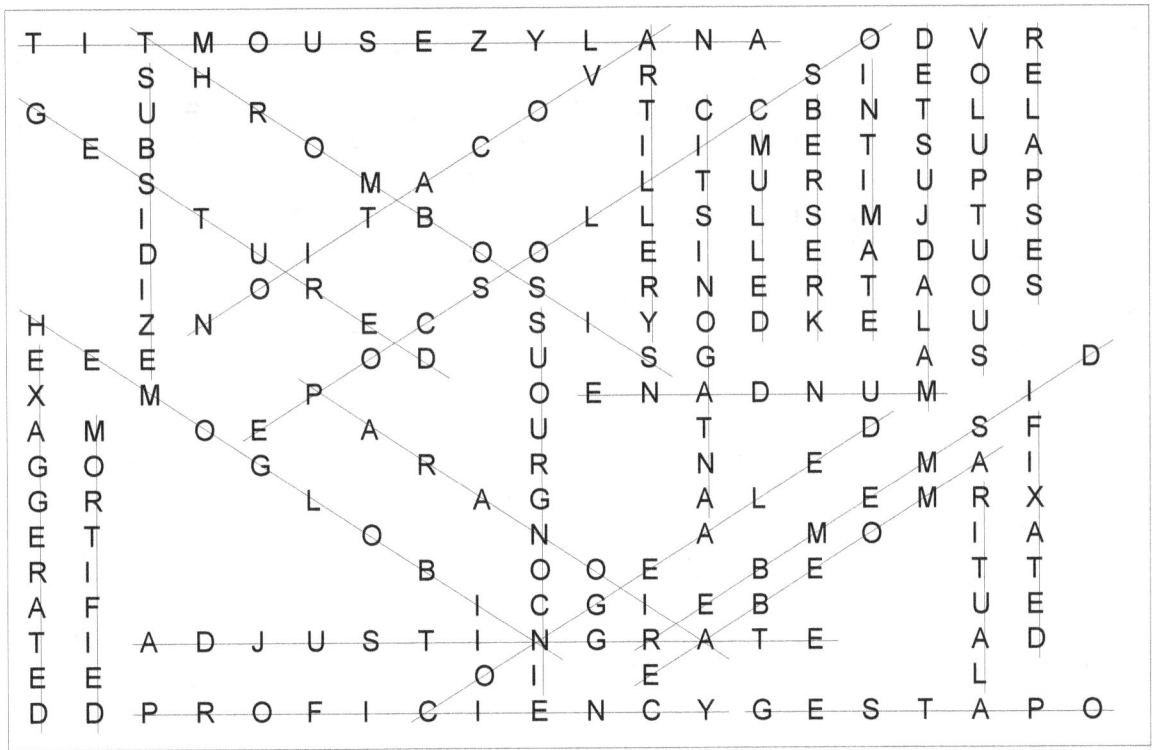

ADJUSTING	FIXATED	MUNDANE
AMOEBAE	GESTAPO	OSCILLOSCOPE
ANALYZE	GESTURED	PARANOIA
ANTAGONISTIC	HEMOGLOBIN	PROFICIENCY
ARTILLERY	INCONGRUOUS	RELAPSES
AVOCATION	INGRATE	RITUAL
BERSERK	INTIMATE	SUBSIDIZE
CONGEALED	MALADJUSTED	THROMBOSIS
DISMEMBER	MORTIFIED	TITMOUSE
EXAGGERATED	MULLED	VOLUPTUOUS

The Pigman Vocabulary Word Search 4

Words are placed backwards, forward, diagonally, up and down. Words listed below are included in the maze. Circle the hidden vocabulary words in the maze.

```
R P C A H E M O G L O B I N S P B C M M
E R O D E T S U J D A L A M U P I O U F
B O N J G P S N H T Y K X Y B T S E N F
M F G U Q F C C T W R Y T N S C P S D X
E I E S K D L H H E C N T I I M E U A C
M C A T E K H N S I E B N L D O T O N K
S I L I Z P M R R C Z O L D I R A M E T
I E E N Y X E W S X G O Z B Z T M T K X
D N D G L B R E Z A S F P K E I I P C
C C G S A Y D D T C V A S H T F T T B T
P Y M R N N Z N O G N V V F R I N S Y S
A I O N A R A P N A M O E B A E I J I K
K V H C L T E G K Q L C Y X M D N S W S
K M N J A D E E D U B A P A V G O I E G
D I K Z U S J S P D D T C Y C B K S C D
F I X A T E D T C J D I P M M X P H E C
P C F U I V U A Z S D O F O S A V L J D
F W R Z R O F P X E F N R C L P L W W B
P E M H U F P O R V H H F E Y U V M S P
D Z Q S B Y J P X M T H R Z M K N Q M F
```

ADJUSTING	GESTURED	PARANOIA
AMOEBAE	HEMOGLOBIN	PREDICAMENT
ANALYZE	INCANDESCENT	PROFICIENCY
ANTAGONISTIC	INGRATE	RELAPSES
AVOCATION	INTIMATE	RITUAL
BERSERK	MALADJUSTED	SCHIZOPHRENIC
CONGEALED	MORTIFIED	SUBSIDIZE
DISMEMBER	MULLED	THROMBOSIS
FIXATED	MUNDANE	TITMOUSE
GESTAPO	OSCILLOSCOPE	VOLUPTUOUS

The Pigman Vocabulary Word Search 4 Answer Key

Words are placed backwards, forward, diagonally, up and down. Words listed below are included in the maze. Circle the hidden vocabulary words in the maze.

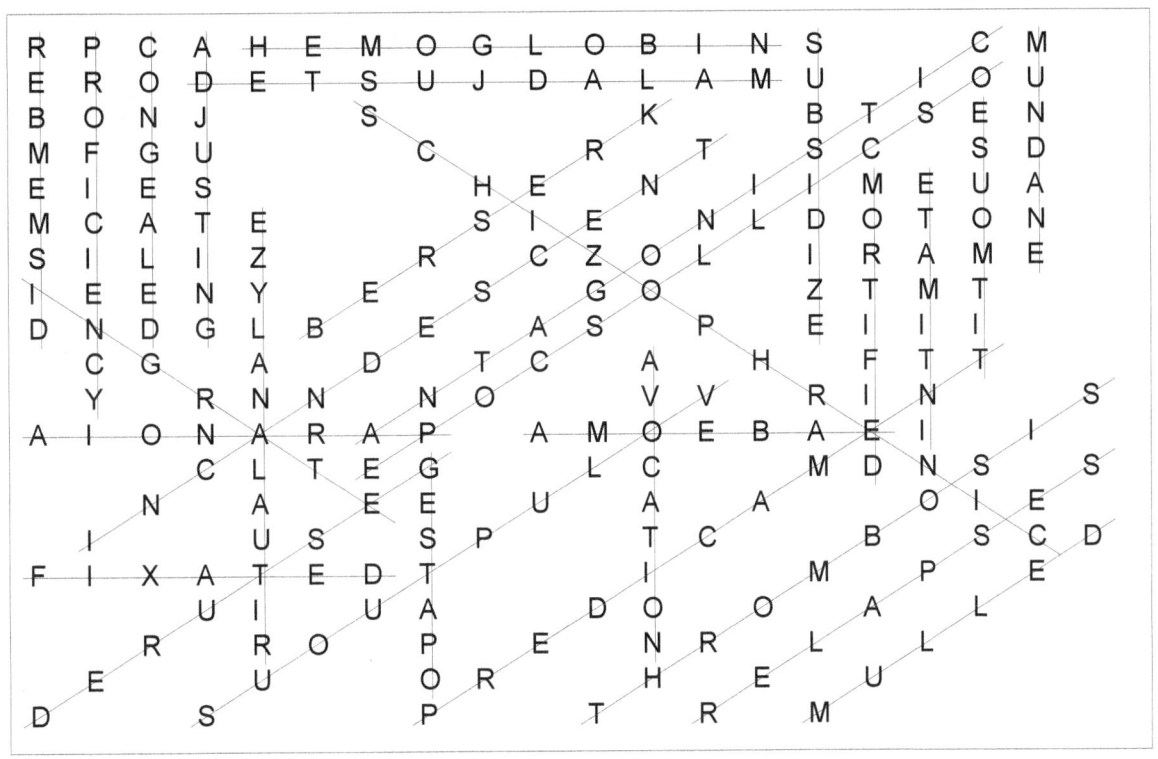

ADJUSTING	GESTURED	PARANOIA
AMOEBAE	HEMOGLOBIN	PREDICAMENT
ANALYZE	INCANDESCENT	PROFICIENCY
ANTAGONISTIC	INGRATE	RELAPSES
AVOCATION	INTIMATE	RITUAL
BERSERK	MALADJUSTED	SCHIZOPHRENIC
CONGEALED	MORTIFIED	SUBSIDIZE
DISMEMBER	MULLED	THROMBOSIS
FIXATED	MUNDANE	TITMOUSE
GESTAPO	OSCILLOSCOPE	VOLUPTUOUS

The Pigman Vocabulary Crossword 1

Across
2. Stuck together; jelled; solidified
7. Close; personal
8. Examine methodically
11. Ordinary; boring
12. Mentally or emotionally upset; deranged
16. To become overly concerned with one subject
18. Divide into pieces
19. Extreme, irrational distrust of others
20. Troublesome situation

Down
1. Ceremony; routine
2. Offset; counterbalance; substitution
3. Fixing to a more compatible position
4. Enlarged or increased to an abnormal degree
5. Thought about; pondered
6. Motioned with hands
7. Incompatible; not belonging together
9. An ungrateful person
10. Presence of a clot in a blood vessel
11. Humiliated; embarrassed
13. Falling back to a former condition
14. Small insect-eating bird
15. Police organization using terroristic methods
17. A microscopic animal in water, soil & as a parasite in other animals

The Pigman Vocabulary Crossword 1 Answer Key

Across
2. Stuck together; jelled; solidified
7. Close; personal
8. Examine methodically
11. Ordinary; boring
12. Mentally or emotionally upset; deranged
16. To become overly concerned with one subject
18. Divide into pieces
19. Extreme, irrational distrust of others
20. Troublesome situation

Down
1. Ceremony; routine
2. Offset; counterbalance; substitution
3. Fixing to a more compatible position
4. Enlarged or increased to an abnormal degree
5. Thought about; pondered
6. Motioned with hands
7. Incompatible; not belonging together
9. An ungrateful person
10. Presence of a clot in a blood vessel
11. Humiliated; embarrassed
13. Falling back to a former condition
14. Small insect-eating bird
15. Police organization using terroristic methods
17. A microscopic animal in water, soil & as a parasite in other animals

The Pigman Vocabulary Crossword 2

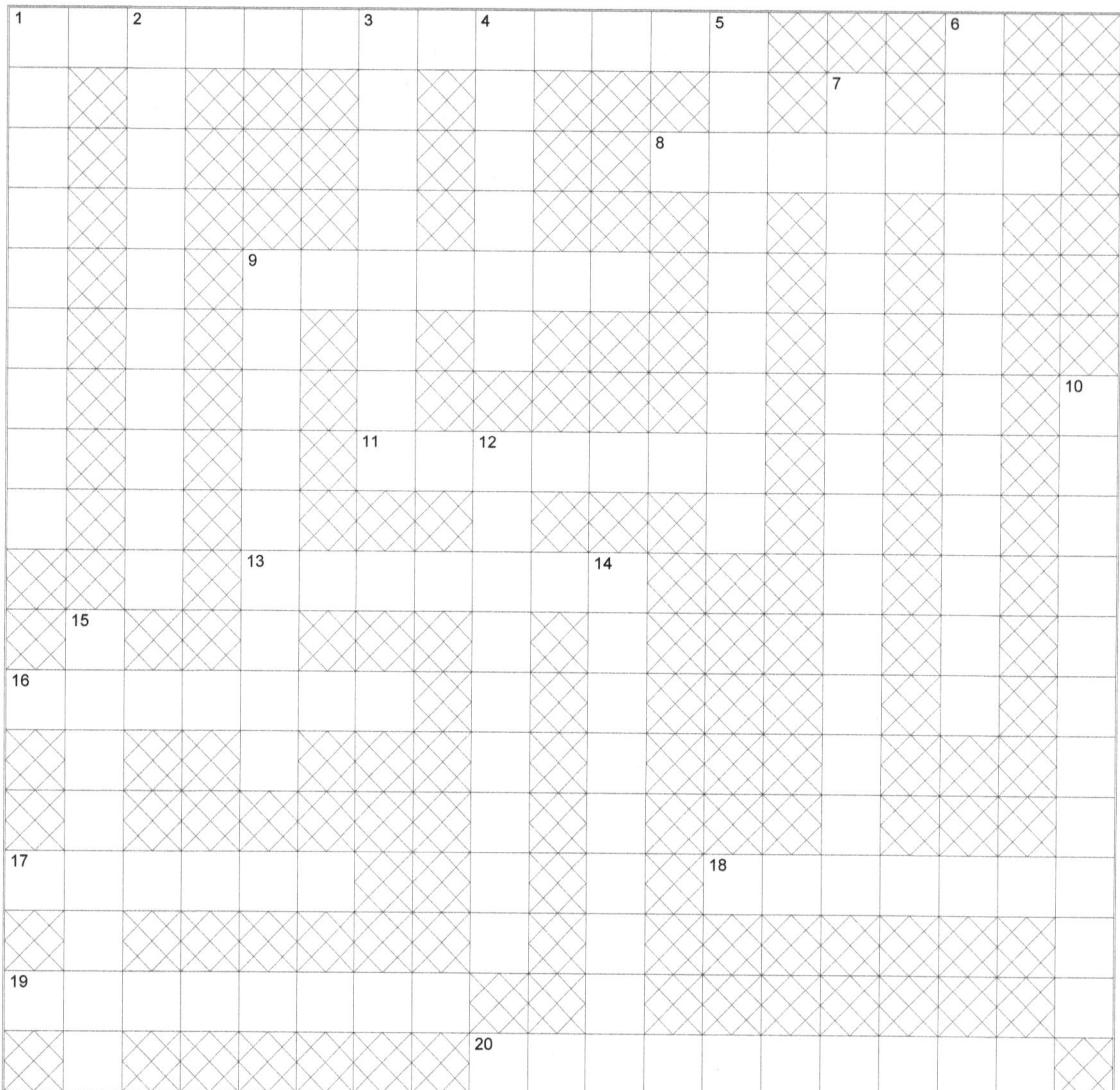

Across
1. Psychological disorder
8. An ungrateful person
9. Ordinary; boring
11. Examine methodically
13. To become overly concerned with one subject
16. Mentally or emotionally upset; deranged
17. Thought about; pondered
18. Police organization using terroristic methods
19. Falling back to a former condition
20. Presence of a clot in a blood vessel

Down
1. Give financial assistance to
2. Iron-containing respiratory pigment in red blood cells
3. Extreme, irrational distrust of others
4. Ceremony; routine
5. Stuck together; jelled; solidified
6. Saying or doing things to intentionally annoy or displease someone
7. Lies; statements straying from the truth
9. Humiliated; embarrassed
10. Incompatible; not belonging together
12. Large caliber weapons
14. Divide into pieces
15. Motioned with hands

The Pigman Vocabulary Crossword 2 Answer Key

	1 S	2 C	H	I	Z	3 O	P	H	4 R	E	N	I	5 C		6 A	
	U		E			P			I				O	7 P	N	
	B		M			A		8 I	N	G	R	A	T	E		
	S		O			R			T				G	E	A	
	I		G	9 M	U	N	D	A	N	E			E	V	G	
	D		L	O		O			L				A	A	O	
	I		O	R		I							L	R	N	10 I
	Z		B	T		11 A	N	12 A	L	Y	Z	E		I	I	N
	E		I	I				R				D		C	S	C
			N	13 F	I	X	A	T	E	14 D				A	T	O
		15 G		I				I		I				T	I	N
	16 B	E	R	S	E	R	K		L		S			I	C	G
		S		D					L		M			O		R
		T							E		E			N		U
	17 M	U	L	L	E	D			R		M		18 G	E	S	T	A	P	O
		R							Y		B					U
	19 R	E	L	A	P	S	E	S		E					S
		D					20 T	H	R	O	M	B	O	S	I	S

Across
1. Psychological disorder
8. An ungrateful person
9. Ordinary; boring
11. Examine methodically
13. To become overly concerned with one subject
16. Mentally or emotionally upset; deranged
17. Thought about; pondered
18. Police organization using terroristic methods
19. Falling back to a former condition
20. Presence of a clot in a blood vessel

Down
1. Give financial assistance to
2. Iron-containing respiratory pigment in red blood cells
3. Extreme, irrational distrust of others
4. Ceremony; routine
5. Stuck together; jelled; solidified
6. Saying or doing things to intentionally annoy or displease someone
7. Lies; statements straying from the truth
9. Humiliated; embarrassed
10. Incompatible; not belonging together
12. Large caliber weapons
14. Divide into pieces
15. Motioned with hands

The Pigman Vocabulary Crossword 3

Across
1. Ceremony; routine
4. Troublesome situation
8. Police organization using terroristic methods
10. Falling back to a former condition
11. Fixing to a more compatible position
14. Examine methodically
16. Enlarged or increased to an abnormal degree
17. Humiliated; embarrassed
18. Thought about; pondered
19. Close; personal

Down
2. An ungrateful person
3. Saying or doing things to intentionally annoy or displease someone
4. Competency; ability to do something well
5. Intentionally; on purpose
6. Stuck together; jelled; solidified
7. Small insect-eating bird
9. Offset; counterbalance; substitution
11. Large caliber weapons
12. Mentally or emotionally upset; deranged
13. Ordinary; boring
14. Hobby; work; profession
15. Motioned with hands

The Pigman Vocabulary Crossword 3 Answer Key

Across
1. Ceremony; routine
4. Troublesome situation
8. Police organization using terroristic methods
10. Falling back to a former condition
11. Fixing to a more compatible position
14. Examine methodically
16. Enlarged or increased to an abnormal degree
17. Humiliated; embarrassed
18. Thought about; pondered
19. Close; personal

Down
2. An ungrateful person
3. Saying or doing things to intentionally annoy or displease someone
4. Competency; ability to do something well
5. Intentionally; on purpose
6. Stuck together; jelled; solidified
7. Small insect-eating bird
9. Offset; counterbalance; substitution
11. Large caliber weapons
12. Mentally or emotionally upset; deranged
13. Ordinary; boring
14. Hobby; work; profession
15. Motioned with hands

The Pigman Vocabulary Crossword 4

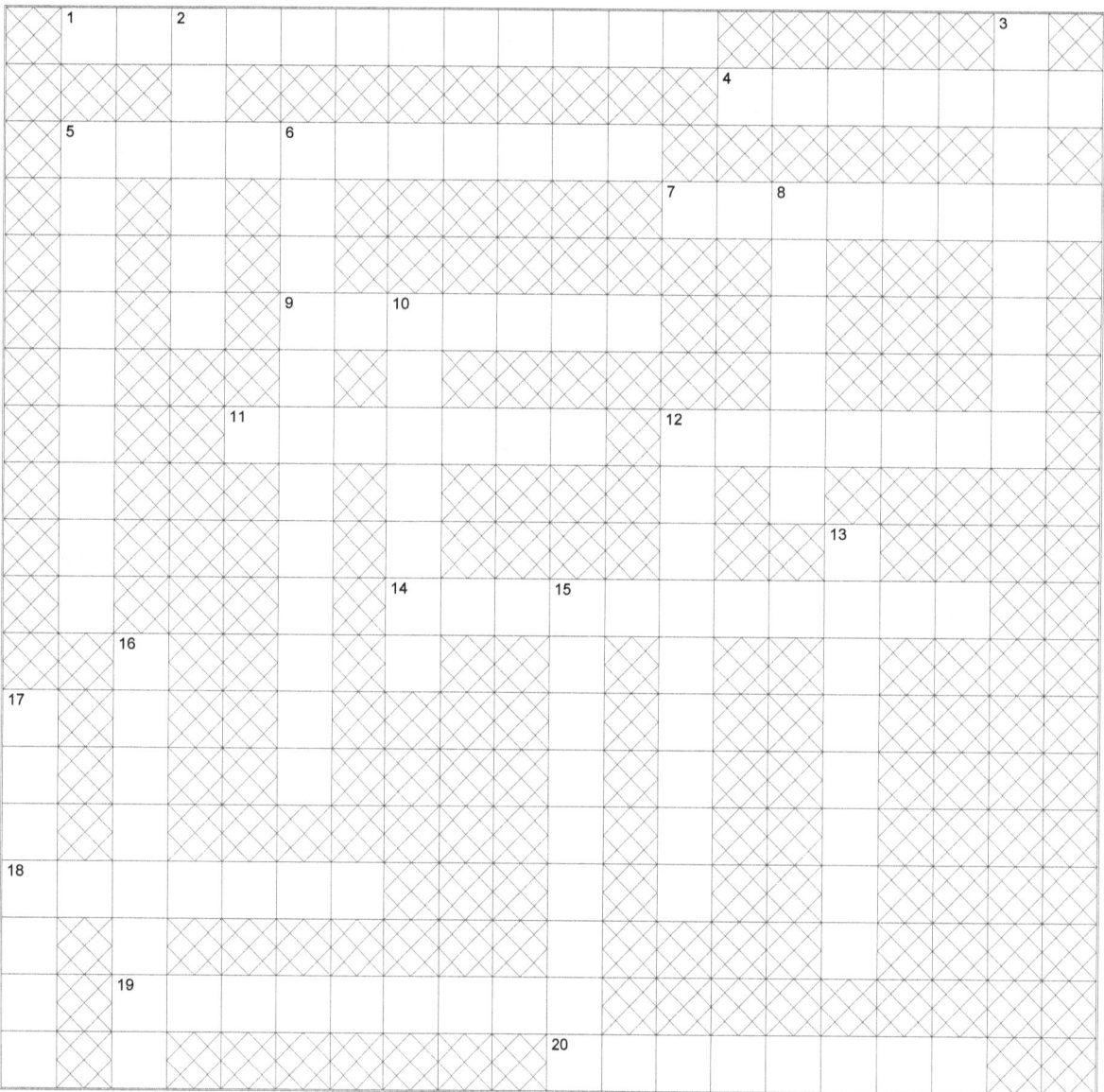

Across
1. Offset; counterbalance; substitution
4. Ordinary; boring
5. Not able to adjust to the demands of personal relationships
7. Extreme, irrational distrust of others
9. An ungrateful person
11. Mentally or emotionally upset; deranged
12. Examine methodically
14. Troublesome situation
18. A microscopic animal in water, soil & as a parasite in other animals
19. Give financial assistance to
20. Falling back to a former condition

Down
2. Thought about; pondered
3. Close; personal
5. Humiliated; embarrassed
6. Intentionally; on purpose
8. Ceremony; routine
10. Police organization using terroristic methods
12. Hobby; work; profession
13. Motioned with hands
15. Divide into pieces
16. Small insect-eating bird
17. To become overly concerned with one subject

The Pigman Vocabulary Crossword 4 Answer Key

Across
1. Offset; counterbalance; substitution
4. Ordinary; boring
5. Not able to adjust to the demands of personal relationships
7. Extreme, irrational distrust of others
9. An ungrateful person
11. Mentally or emotionally upset; deranged
12. Examine methodically
14. Troublesome situation
18. A microscopic animal in water, soil & as a parasite in other animals
19. Give financial assistance to
20. Falling back to a former condition

Down
2. Thought about; pondered
3. Close; personal
5. Humiliated; embarrassed
6. Intentionally; on purpose
8. Ceremony; routine
10. Police organization using terroristic methods
12. Hobby; work; profession
13. Motioned with hands
15. Divide into pieces
16. Small insect-eating bird
17. To become overly concerned with one subject

The Pigman Vocabulary Juggle Letters 1

1. OTOCMNPEANIS = 1. _____
   Offset; counterbalance; substitution

2. GLNEECAOD = 2. _____
   Stuck together; jelled; solidified

3. RTREALLIY = 3. _____
   Large caliber weapons

4. ESICOLOSPCOL = 4. _____
   Electronic instrument that shows movements of voltage & currents

5. AICGSNNAOTTI = 5. _____
   Saying or doing things to intentionally annoy or displease someone

6. UVPOOTLUUS = 6. _____
   Giving ample, unrestrained pleasure to the senses

7. LMLUED = 7. _____
   Thought about; pondered

8. SROONUGCINU = 8. _____
   Incompatible; not belonging together

9. CATOIOVAN = 9. _____
   Hobby; work; profession

10. TSETOUMI =10. _____
    Small insect-eating bird

11. RHSZCIPNECOIH =11. _____
    Psychological disorder

12. MATITINE =12. _____
    Close; personal

13. DUSJNGITA =13. _____
    Fixing to a more compatible position

14. ARGXEEGEATD =14. _____
    Enlarged or increased to an abnormal degree

15. BSHROMSOIT =15. _____
    Presence of a clot in a blood vessel

The Pigman Vocabulary Juggle Letters 1 Answer Key

1. OTOCMNPEANIS = 1. COMPENSATION
   Offset; counterbalance; substitution

2. GLNEECAOD = 2. CONGEALED
   Stuck together; jelled; solidified

3. RTREALLIY = 3. ARTILLERY
   Large caliber weapons

4. ESICOLOSPCOL = 4. OSCILLOSCOPE
   Electronic instrument that shows movements of voltage & currents

5. AICGSNNAOTTI = 5. ANTAGONISTIC
   Saying or doing things to intentionally annoy or displease someone

6. UVPOOTLUUS = 6. VOLUPTUOUS
   Giving ample, unrestrained pleasure to the senses

7. LMLUED = 7. MULLED
   Thought about; pondered

8. SROONUGCINU = 8. INCONGRUOUS
   Incompatible; not belonging together

9. CATOIOVAN = 9. AVOCATION
   Hobby; work; profession

10. TSETOUMI = 10. TITMOUSE
    Small insect-eating bird

11. RHSZCIPNECOIH = 11. SCHIZOPHRENIC
    Psychological disorder

12. MATITINE = 12. INTIMATE
    Close; personal

13. DUSJNGITA = 13. ADJUSTING
    Fixing to a more compatible position

14. ARGXEEGEATD = 14. EXAGGERATED
    Enlarged or increased to an abnormal degree

15. BSHROMSOIT = 15. THROMBOSIS
    Presence of a clot in a blood vessel

Copyrighted

The Pigman Vocabulary Juggle Letters 2

1. RIANTEG = 1. _____
   An ungrateful person

2. TXFDIEA = 2. _____
   To become overly concerned with one subject

3. AEUSLJTDDAM = 3. _____
   Not able to adjust to the demands of personal relationships

4. PUVOULSTUO = 4. _____
   Giving ample, unrestrained pleasure to the senses

5. DLUMLE = 5. _____
   Thought about; pondered

6. ENIMIATT = 6. _____
   Close; personal

7. NNOICASAITTG = 7. _____
   Saying or doing things to intentionally annoy or displease someone

8. CIENNNCSDTAE = 8. _____
   Giving off visible light as a result of being heated

9. ACEENODLG = 9. _____
   Stuck together; jelled; solidified

10. IMTDOFIRE =10. _____
    Humiliated; embarrassed

11. UTEMOTSI =11. _____
    Small insect-eating bird

12. TEMRPECINDA =12. _____
    Troublesome situation

13. EMNNDUA =13. _____
    Ordinary; boring

14. SUEERDGT =14. _____
    Motioned with hands

15. ROAAIANP =15. _____
    Extreme, irrational distrust of others

The Pigman Vocabulary Juggle Letters 2 Answer Key

1. RIANTEG = 1. INGRATE
   An ungrateful person

2. TXFDIEA = 2. FIXATED
   To become overly concerned with one subject

3. AEUSLJTDDAM = 3. MALADJUSTED
   Not able to adjust to the demands of personal relationships

4. PUVOULSTUO = 4. VOLUPTUOUS
   Giving ample, unrestrained pleasure to the senses

5. DLUMLE = 5. MULLED
   Thought about; pondered

6. ENIMIATT = 6. INTIMATE
   Close; personal

7. NNOICASAITTG = 7. ANTAGONISTIC
   Saying or doing things to intentionally annoy or displease someone

8. CIENNNCSDTAE = 8. INCANDESCENT
   Giving off visible light as a result of being heated

9. ACEENODLG = 9. CONGEALED
   Stuck together; jelled; solidified

10. IMTDOFIRE = 10. MORTIFIED
    Humiliated; embarrassed

11. UTEMOTSI = 11. TITMOUSE
    Small insect-eating bird

12. TEMRPECINDA = 12. PREDICAMENT
    Troublesome situation

13. EMNNDUA = 13. MUNDANE
    Ordinary; boring

14. SUEERDGT = 14. GESTURED
    Motioned with hands

15. ROAAIANP = 15. PARANOIA
    Extreme, irrational distrust of others

The Pigman Vocabulary Juggle Letters 3

1. NITCAOSGITAN = 1. _____
   Saying or doing things to intentionally annoy or displease someone

2. SUNRGIOCUNO = 2. _____
   Incompatible; not belonging together

3. TERLYAILR = 3. _____
   Large caliber weapons

4. TAPIMCOSEONN = 4. _____
   Offset; counterbalance; substitution

5. SUIIBDESZ = 5. _____
   Give financial assistance to

6. HSBTSOMROI = 6. _____
   Presence of a clot in a blood vessel

7. ERGDSTUE = 7. _____
   Motioned with hands

8. YLLIBAREDEET = 8. _____
   Intentionally; on purpose

9. DLMLEU = 9. _____
   Thought about; pondered

10. BAMEOAE = 10. _____
    A microscopic animal in water, soil & as a parasite in other animals

11. BNLEGHOOIM = 11. _____
    Iron-containing respiratory pigment in red blood cells

12. ANARPIOA = 12. _____
    Extreme, irrational distrust of others

13. MOUTTISE = 13. _____
    Small insect-eating bird

14. TNEMTAII = 14. _____
    Close; personal

15. ETSAGOP = 15. _____
    Police organization using terroristic methods

The Pigman Vocabulary Juggle Letters 3 Answer Key

1. NITCAOSGITAN = 1. ANTAGONISTIC
   Saying or doing things to intentionally annoy or displease someone

2. SUNRGIOCUNO = 2. INCONGRUOUS
   Incompatible; not belonging together

3. TERLYAILR = 3. ARTILLERY
   Large caliber weapons

4. TAPIMCOSEONN = 4. COMPENSATION
   Offset; counterbalance; substitution

5. SUIIBDESZ = 5. SUBSIDIZE
   Give financial assistance to

6. HSBTSOMROI = 6. THROMBOSIS
   Presence of a clot in a blood vessel

7. ERGDSTUE = 7. GESTURED
   Motioned with hands

8. YLLIBAREDEET = 8. DELIBERATELY
   Intentionally; on purpose

9. DLMLEU = 9. MULLED
   Thought about; pondered

10. BAMEOAE = 10. AMOEBAE
    A microscopic animal in water, soil & as a parasite in other animals

11. BNLEGHOOIM = 11. HEMOGLOBIN
    Iron-containing respiratory pigment in red blood cells

12. ANARPIOA = 12. PARANOIA
    Extreme, irrational distrust of others

13. MOUTTISE = 13. TITMOUSE
    Small insect-eating bird

14. TNEMTAII = 14. INTIMATE
    Close; personal

15. ETSAGOP = 15. GESTAPO
    Police organization using terroristic methods

The Pigman Vocabulary Juggle Letters 4

1. NRATIRICVSOPAE = 1. _____
   Lies; statements straying from the truth

2. ANUENMD = 2. _____
   Ordinary; boring

3. CNTAOVIAO = 3. _____
   Hobby; work; profession

4. USNGJDTAI = 4. _____
   Fixing to a more compatible position

5. OAPRAINA = 5. _____
   Extreme, irrational distrust of others

6. ATGAEXEREDG = 6. _____
   Enlarged or increased to an abnormal degree

7. OMTOHSIBRS = 7. _____
   Presence of a clot in a blood vessel

8. TCOAIAGNNSIT = 8. _____
   Saying or doing things to intentionally annoy or displease someone

9. ITMANEIT = 9. _____
   Close; personal

10. OBEGHNLMOI =10. _____
    Iron-containing respiratory pigment in red blood cells

11. CHZINSOPIHCRE =11. _____
    Psychological disorder

12. PONSEOCTNAMI =12. _____
    Offset; counterbalance; substitution

13. AENDETCNNSIC =13. _____
    Giving off visible light as a result of being heated

14. SRPLAEES =14. _____
    Falling back to a former condition

15. RAGTNIE =15. _____
    An ungrateful person

The Pigman Vocabulary Juggle Letters 4 Answer Key

1. NRATIRICVSOPAE = 1. PREVARICATIONS
   Lies; statements straying from the truth

2. ANUENMD = 2. MUNDANE
   Ordinary; boring

3. CNTAOVIAO = 3. AVOCATION
   Hobby; work; profession

4. USNGJDTAI = 4. ADJUSTING
   Fixing to a more compatible position

5. OAPRAINA = 5. PARANOIA
   Extreme, irrational distrust of others

6. ATGAEXEREDG = 6. EXAGGERATED
   Enlarged or increased to an abnormal degree

7. OMTOHSIBRS = 7. THROMBOSIS
   Presence of a clot in a blood vessel

8. TCOAIAGNNSIT = 8. ANTAGONISTIC
   Saying or doing things to intentionally annoy or displease someone

9. ITMANEIT = 9. INTIMATE
   Close; personal

10. OBEGHNLMOI = 10. HEMOGLOBIN
    Iron-containing respiratory pigment in red blood cells

11. CHZINSOPIHCRE = 11. SCHIZOPHRENIC
    Psychological disorder

12. PONSEOCTNAMI = 12. COMPENSATION
    Offset; counterbalance; substitution

13. AENDETCNNSIC = 13. INCANDESCENT
    Giving off visible light as a result of being heated

14. SRPLAEES = 14. RELAPSES
    Falling back to a former condition

15. RAGTNIE = 15. INGRATE
    An ungrateful person

ADJUSTING	Fixing to a more compatible position
AMOEBAE	A microscopic animal in water, soil & as a parasite in other animals
ANALYZE	Examine methodically
ANTAGONISTIC	Saying or doing things to intentionally annoy or displease someone
ARTILLERY	Large caliber weapons
AVOCATION	Hobby; work; profession

BERSERK	Mentally or emotionally upset; deranged
COMPENSATION	Offset; counterbalance; substitution
CONGEALED	Stuck together; jelled; solidified
DELIBERATELY	Intentionally; on purpose
DISMEMBER	Divide into pieces
EXAGGERATED	Enlarged or increased to an abnormal degree

FIXATED	To become overly concerned with one subject
GESTAPO	Police organization using terroristic methods
GESTURED	Motioned with hands
HEMOGLOBIN	Iron-containing respiratory pigment in red blood cells
INCANDESCENT	Giving off visible light as a result of being heated
INCONGRUOUS	Incompatible; not belonging together

INGRATE	An ungrateful person
INTIMATE	Close; personal
MALADJUSTED	Not able to adjust to the demands of personal relationships
MORTIFIED	Humiliated; embarrassed
MULLED	Thought about; pondered
MUNDANE	Ordinary; boring

OSCILLOSCOPE	Electronic instrument that shows movements of voltage & currents
PARANOIA	Extreme, irrational distrust of others
PREDICAMENT	Troublesome situation
PREVARICATIONS	Lies; statements straying from the truth
PROFICIENCY	Competency; ability to do something well
RELAPSES	Falling back to a former condition

RITUAL	Ceremony; routine
SCHIZOPHRENIC	Psychological disorder
SUBSIDIZE	Give financial assistance to
THROMBOSIS	Presence of a clot in a blood vessel
TITMOUSE	Small insect-eating bird
VOLUPTUOUS	Giving ample, unrestrained pleasure to the senses

The Pigman Vocabulary

INTIMATE	GESTURED	PREDICAMENT	PARANOIA	ADJUSTING
INCONGRUOUS	OSCILLOSCOPE	FIXATED	THROMBOSIS	INGRATE
MORTIFIED	VOLUPTUOUS	FREE SPACE	BERSERK	EXAGGERATED
INCANDESCENT	MULLED	COMPENSATION	SUBSIDIZE	PROFICIENCY
CONGEALED	RITUAL	PREVARICATIONS	SCHIZOPHRENIC	DELIBERATELY

The Pigman Vocabulary

ANTAGONISTIC	DISMEMBER	ARTILLERY	RELAPSES	AMOEBAE
MUNDANE	AVOCATION	MALADJUSTED	GESTAPO	HEMOGLOBIN
TITMOUSE	DELIBERATELY	FREE SPACE	PREVARICATIONS	RITUAL
CONGEALED	PROFICIENCY	SUBSIDIZE	COMPENSATION	MULLED
INCANDESCENT	EXAGGERATED	BERSERK	ANALYZE	VOLUPTUOUS

The Pigman Vocabulary

COMPENSATION	ANALYZE	PARANOIA	HEMOGLOBIN	EXAGGERATED
DISMEMBER	PROFICIENCY	CONGEALED	AMOEBAE	OSCILLOSCOPE
TITMOUSE	MORTIFIED	FREE SPACE	RITUAL	GESTURED
MALADJUSTED	ANTAGONISTIC	BERSERK	THROMBOSIS	INCONGRUOUS
SUBSIDIZE	PREVARICATIONS	AVOCATION	VOLUPTUOUS	MULLED

The Pigman Vocabulary

GESTAPO	ARTILLERY	DELIBERATELY	INCANDESCENT	FIXATED
INTIMATE	INGRATE	SCHIZOPHRENIC	PREDICAMENT	RELAPSES
ADJUSTING	MULLED	FREE SPACE	AVOCATION	PREVARICATIONS
SUBSIDIZE	INCONGRUOUS	THROMBOSIS	BERSERK	ANTAGONISTIC
MALADJUSTED	GESTURED	RITUAL	MUNDANE	MORTIFIED

The Pigman Vocabulary

HEMOGLOBIN	RELAPSES	RITUAL	AVOCATION	OSCILLOSCOPE
INCANDESCENT	THROMBOSIS	MULLED	PROFICIENCY	PREVARICATIONS
PREDICAMENT	INCONGRUOUS	FREE SPACE	VOLUPTUOUS	MORTIFIED
COMPENSATION	DELIBERATELY	PARANOIA	DISMEMBER	BERSERK
GESTAPO	GESTURED	ANTAGONISTIC	ADJUSTING	FIXATED

The Pigman Vocabulary

ANALYZE	SUBSIDIZE	INGRATE	ARTILLERY	INTIMATE
TITMOUSE	EXAGGERATED	CONGEALED	SCHIZOPHRENIC	AMOEBAE
MUNDANE	FIXATED	FREE SPACE	ANTAGONISTIC	GESTURED
GESTAPO	BERSERK	DISMEMBER	PARANOIA	DELIBERATELY
COMPENSATION	MORTIFIED	VOLUPTUOUS	MALADJUSTED	INCONGRUOUS

The Pigman Vocabulary

TITMOUSE	EXAGGERATED	PARANOIA	MULLED	DELIBERATELY
HEMOGLOBIN	ANALYZE	INCONGRUOUS	ADJUSTING	ANTAGONISTIC
OSCILLOSCOPE	COMPENSATION	FREE SPACE	CONGEALED	DISMEMBER
AMOEBAE	ARTILLERY	FIXATED	BERSERK	INTIMATE
RELAPSES	GESTAPO	PROFICIENCY	INGRATE	SCHIZOPHRENIC

The Pigman Vocabulary

INCANDESCENT	THROMBOSIS	MORTIFIED	PREDICAMENT	RITUAL
AVOCATION	VOLUPTUOUS	SUBSIDIZE	MALADJUSTED	PREVARICATIONS
GESTURED	SCHIZOPHRENIC	FREE SPACE	PROFICIENCY	GESTAPO
RELAPSES	INTIMATE	BERSERK	FIXATED	ARTILLERY
AMOEBAE	DISMEMBER	CONGEALED	MUNDANE	COMPENSATION

The Pigman Vocabulary

MORTIFIED	GESTURED	PREVARICATIONS	INCONGRUOUS	DISMEMBER
AMOEBAE	THROMBOSIS	COMPENSATION	INCANDESCENT	SCHIZOPHRENIC
GESTAPO	ADJUSTING	FREE SPACE	ANTAGONISTIC	HEMOGLOBIN
INGRATE	RITUAL	FIXATED	TITMOUSE	OSCILLOSCOPE
PROFICIENCY	SUBSIDIZE	ARTILLERY	ANALYZE	MUNDANE

The Pigman Vocabulary

VOLUPTUOUS	BERSERK	PARANOIA	AVOCATION	PREDICAMENT
INTIMATE	RELAPSES	MULLED	CONGEALED	DELIBERATELY
MALADJUSTED	MUNDANE	FREE SPACE	ARTILLERY	SUBSIDIZE
PROFICIENCY	OSCILLOSCOPE	TITMOUSE	FIXATED	RITUAL
INGRATE	HEMOGLOBIN	ANTAGONISTIC	EXAGGERATED	ADJUSTING

The Pigman Vocabulary

MALADJUSTED	RELAPSES	SCHIZOPHRENIC	PARANOIA	SUBSIDIZE
HEMOGLOBIN	AMOEBAE	GESTAPO	GESTURED	ADJUSTING
INGRATE	DELIBERATELY	FREE SPACE	OSCILLOSCOPE	RITUAL
ANTAGONISTIC	AVOCATION	CONGEALED	BERSERK	PREVARICATIONS
ANALYZE	TITMOUSE	MORTIFIED	INCANDESCENT	MULLED

The Pigman Vocabulary

FIXATED	MUNDANE	VOLUPTUOUS	THROMBOSIS	INCONGRUOUS
INTIMATE	PREDICAMENT	EXAGGERATED	ARTILLERY	COMPENSATION
DISMEMBER	MULLED	FREE SPACE	MORTIFIED	TITMOUSE
ANALYZE	PREVARICATIONS	BERSERK	CONGEALED	AVOCATION
ANTAGONISTIC	RITUAL	OSCILLOSCOPE	PROFICIENCY	DELIBERATELY

The Pigman Vocabulary

THROMBOSIS	GESTAPO	DISMEMBER	EXAGGERATED	RITUAL
INTIMATE	FIXATED	ANTAGONISTIC	ARTILLERY	SCHIZOPHRENIC
MORTIFIED	TITMOUSE	FREE SPACE	INCANDESCENT	BERSERK
HEMOGLOBIN	COMPENSATION	ADJUSTING	INGRATE	INCONGRUOUS
AMOEBAE	PREDICAMENT	DELIBERATELY	RELAPSES	CONGEALED

The Pigman Vocabulary

MUNDANE	MALADJUSTED	ANALYZE	AVOCATION	PREVARICATIONS
VOLUPTUOUS	PARANOIA	MULLED	GESTURED	OSCILLOSCOPE
PROFICIENCY	CONGEALED	FREE SPACE	DELIBERATELY	PREDICAMENT
AMOEBAE	INCONGRUOUS	INGRATE	ADJUSTING	COMPENSATION
HEMOGLOBIN	BERSERK	INCANDESCENT	SUBSIDIZE	TITMOUSE

The Pigman Vocabulary

DELIBERATELY	SCHIZOPHRENIC	COMPENSATION	INCONGRUOUS	AMOEBAE
GESTAPO	TITMOUSE	CONGEALED	THROMBOSIS	ARTILLERY
PROFICIENCY	MUNDANE	FREE SPACE	SUBSIDIZE	PREDICAMENT
OSCILLOSCOPE	ADJUSTING	ANTAGONISTIC	HEMOGLOBIN	PARANOIA
BERSERK	FIXATED	MORTIFIED	ANALYZE	PREVARICATIONS

The Pigman Vocabulary

RITUAL	MULLED	VOLUPTUOUS	MALADJUSTED	GESTURED
AVOCATION	EXAGGERATED	INGRATE	DISMEMBER	INCANDESCENT
RELAPSES	PREVARICATIONS	FREE SPACE	MORTIFIED	FIXATED
BERSERK	PARANOIA	HEMOGLOBIN	ANTAGONISTIC	ADJUSTING
OSCILLOSCOPE	PREDICAMENT	SUBSIDIZE	INTIMATE	MUNDANE

The Pigman Vocabulary

MULLED	DELIBERATELY	PROFICIENCY	BERSERK	OSCILLOSCOPE
AMOEBAE	CONGEALED	RELAPSES	FIXATED	RITUAL
INTIMATE	PREDICAMENT	FREE SPACE	MORTIFIED	SCHIZOPHRENIC
ANTAGONISTIC	EXAGGERATED	PREVARICATIONS	ADJUSTING	COMPENSATION
MALADJUSTED	GESTAPO	INCANDESCENT	SUBSIDIZE	TITMOUSE

The Pigman Vocabulary

PARANOIA	INCONGRUOUS	THROMBOSIS	VOLUPTUOUS	ARTILLERY
AVOCATION	HEMOGLOBIN	GESTURED	MUNDANE	ANALYZE
DISMEMBER	TITMOUSE	FREE SPACE	INCANDESCENT	GESTAPO
MALADJUSTED	COMPENSATION	ADJUSTING	PREVARICATIONS	EXAGGERATED
ANTAGONISTIC	SCHIZOPHRENIC	MORTIFIED	INGRATE	PREDICAMENT

The Pigman Vocabulary

DISMEMBER	ARTILLERY	RELAPSES	SCHIZOPHRENIC	SUBSIDIZE
MUNDANE	ANTAGONISTIC	EXAGGERATED	GESTAPO	PARANOIA
HEMOGLOBIN	FIXATED	FREE SPACE	AVOCATION	DELIBERATELY
INTIMATE	VOLUPTUOUS	INGRATE	PREDICAMENT	AMOEBAE
INCANDESCENT	PROFICIENCY	INCONGRUOUS	GESTURED	COMPENSATION

The Pigman Vocabulary

THROMBOSIS	PREVARICATIONS	CONGEALED	TITMOUSE	ADJUSTING
OSCILLOSCOPE	MALADJUSTED	ANALYZE	RITUAL	MULLED
BERSERK	COMPENSATION	FREE SPACE	INCONGRUOUS	PROFICIENCY
INCANDESCENT	AMOEBAE	PREDICAMENT	INGRATE	VOLUPTUOUS
INTIMATE	DELIBERATELY	AVOCATION	MORTIFIED	FIXATED

The Pigman Vocabulary

FIXATED	MALADJUSTED	GESTURED	CONGEALED	DELIBERATELY
PREDICAMENT	INCONGRUOUS	MORTIFIED	ARTILLERY	INCANDESCENT
RELAPSES	AMOEBAE	FREE SPACE	OSCILLOSCOPE	SCHIZOPHRENIC
EXAGGERATED	ANTAGONISTIC	INTIMATE	TITMOUSE	COMPENSATION
SUBSIDIZE	AVOCATION	PARANOIA	PREVARICATIONS	INGRATE

The Pigman Vocabulary

PROFICIENCY	BERSERK	ANALYZE	MULLED	MUNDANE
ADJUSTING	THROMBOSIS	HEMOGLOBIN	VOLUPTUOUS	GESTAPO
DISMEMBER	INGRATE	FREE SPACE	PARANOIA	AVOCATION
SUBSIDIZE	COMPENSATION	TITMOUSE	INTIMATE	ANTAGONISTIC
EXAGGERATED	SCHIZOPHRENIC	OSCILLOSCOPE	RITUAL	AMOEBAE

The Pigman Vocabulary

FIXATED	INGRATE	AMOEBAE	AVOCATION	OSCILLOSCOPE
ADJUSTING	PROFICIENCY	PARANOIA	DELIBERATELY	BERSERK
SUBSIDIZE	MALADJUSTED	FREE SPACE	COMPENSATION	RELAPSES
ARTILLERY	MULLED	MUNDANE	SCHIZOPHRENIC	GESTURED
MORTIFIED	TITMOUSE	PREVARICATIONS	DISMEMBER	ANALYZE

The Pigman Vocabulary

RITUAL	CONGEALED	INTIMATE	HEMOGLOBIN	VOLUPTUOUS
INCONGRUOUS	GESTAPO	INCANDESCENT	ANTAGONISTIC	THROMBOSIS
EXAGGERATED	ANALYZE	FREE SPACE	PREVARICATIONS	TITMOUSE
MORTIFIED	GESTURED	SCHIZOPHRENIC	MUNDANE	MULLED
ARTILLERY	RELAPSES	COMPENSATION	PREDICAMENT	MALADJUSTED

The Pigman Vocabulary

MULLED	ARTILLERY	RELAPSES	INCONGRUOUS	COMPENSATION
ADJUSTING	ANTAGONISTIC	GESTAPO	SUBSIDIZE	PROFICIENCY
FIXATED	CONGEALED	FREE SPACE	PARANOIA	PREDICAMENT
MALADJUSTED	DELIBERATELY	MUNDANE	SCHIZOPHRENIC	AVOCATION
GESTURED	PREVARICATIONS	OSCILLOSCOPE	VOLUPTUOUS	ANALYZE

The Pigman Vocabulary

INCANDESCENT	BERSERK	THROMBOSIS	MORTIFIED	HEMOGLOBIN
DISMEMBER	RITUAL	TITMOUSE	EXAGGERATED	INGRATE
AMOEBAE	ANALYZE	FREE SPACE	OSCILLOSCOPE	PREVARICATIONS
GESTURED	AVOCATION	SCHIZOPHRENIC	MUNDANE	DELIBERATELY
MALADJUSTED	PREDICAMENT	PARANOIA	INTIMATE	CONGEALED

The Pigman Vocabulary

HEMOGLOBIN	OSCILLOSCOPE	INGRATE	GESTURED	ADJUSTING
FIXATED	TITMOUSE	AVOCATION	RELAPSES	VOLUPTUOUS
PROFICIENCY	MUNDANE	FREE SPACE	PREDICAMENT	PREVARICATIONS
DISMEMBER	ARTILLERY	INCONGRUOUS	ANTAGONISTIC	PARANOIA
BERSERK	THROMBOSIS	DELIBERATELY	AMOEBAE	INTIMATE

The Pigman Vocabulary

MALADJUSTED	SUBSIDIZE	EXAGGERATED	RITUAL	COMPENSATION
MULLED	GESTAPO	CONGEALED	SCHIZOPHRENIC	MORTIFIED
ANALYZE	INTIMATE	FREE SPACE	DELIBERATELY	THROMBOSIS
BERSERK	PARANOIA	ANTAGONISTIC	INCONGRUOUS	ARTILLERY
DISMEMBER	PREVARICATIONS	PREDICAMENT	INCANDESCENT	MUNDANE

The Pigman Vocabulary

PREVARICATIONS	INCONGRUOUS	COMPENSATION	EXAGGERATED	ANTAGONISTIC
INTIMATE	AVOCATION	ARTILLERY	GESTAPO	AMOEBAE
MUNDANE	THROMBOSIS	FREE SPACE	PROFICIENCY	MALADJUSTED
ANALYZE	DELIBERATELY	RELAPSES	BERSERK	OSCILLOSCOPE
MORTIFIED	HEMOGLOBIN	SCHIZOPHRENIC	PREDICAMENT	PARANOIA

The Pigman Vocabulary

RITUAL	VOLUPTUOUS	DISMEMBER	INGRATE	FIXATED
TITMOUSE	INCANDESCENT	SUBSIDIZE	CONGEALED	ADJUSTING
MULLED	PARANOIA	FREE SPACE	SCHIZOPHRENIC	HEMOGLOBIN
MORTIFIED	OSCILLOSCOPE	BERSERK	RELAPSES	DELIBERATELY
ANALYZE	MALADJUSTED	PROFICIENCY	GESTURED	THROMBOSIS

The Pigman Vocabulary

TITMOUSE	INTIMATE	THROMBOSIS	GESTAPO	AMOEBAE
RELAPSES	RITUAL	VOLUPTUOUS	GESTURED	EXAGGERATED
INCONGRUOUS	DELIBERATELY	FREE SPACE	MUNDANE	COMPENSATION
PREDICAMENT	SUBSIDIZE	ARTILLERY	HEMOGLOBIN	INGRATE
MORTIFIED	ADJUSTING	MULLED	PARANOIA	DISMEMBER

The Pigman Vocabulary

ANTAGONISTIC	INCANDESCENT	CONGEALED	PROFICIENCY	ANALYZE
MALADJUSTED	AVOCATION	FIXATED	BERSERK	SCHIZOPHRENIC
PREVARICATIONS	DISMEMBER	FREE SPACE	MULLED	ADJUSTING
MORTIFIED	INGRATE	HEMOGLOBIN	ARTILLERY	SUBSIDIZE
PREDICAMENT	COMPENSATION	MUNDANE	OSCILLOSCOPE	DELIBERATELY

www.ingramcontent.com/pod-product-compliance
Lightning Source LLC
Chambersburg PA
CBHW081458070526
44586CB00019B/2413